SERVICE REBORN

The Knowledge, Skills, and Attitudes of Service Companies

A Conversation with
Po Chung

Co-founder, DHL International, Asia Pacific
Chairman Emeritus, DHL Express (Hong Kong) Limited
Chairman, Hong Kong Institute of Service
Leadership & Management

as interviewed by
Art Bell, PhD, Business Editor, Lexingford Publishing

ISBN-978-0-984493883
Library of Congress No. 2012942280
Publication Date: June 20, 2012 First Edition

L

Lexingford Publishing
New York
San Francisco
Hong Kong

www.lexingfordpublishing.yolasite.com

Preface

Like many of life's happy accidents, the conversations that eventually linked together to make up this book began as chat between friends. Art Bell was visiting Hong Kong for a year as columnist for the *South China Morning Post* and an administrator in the School of Business at Hong Kong University of Science and Technology. I was deeply involved in the "3-3-4" conversion of Hong Kong's major universities to include a fourth year of study emphasizing the liberal arts. As Art and I discussed university curricula both in Hong Kong and the U.S., it became increasingly clear to me that a golden opportunity was at hand: Hong Kong could lead the way in educating students for their likely future careers in service occupations and companies. More than 90 percent of Hong Kong's current GDP, after all, springs from the service sector rather than manufacturing. Nevertheless, no one had delineated for universities and other schools how to best prepare students as service leaders. Although there were courses aplenty in product-oriented studies, few universities if any offered courses geared to the vast majority of their students who would find employment in service roles.

Our conversations focused, therefore, on how to understand the "DNA" or core nature of service organizations and, just as important, how to prepare oneself and others to be service leaders. Ideas and best practices that I had "lived" in my own professional life as a corporate leader at

DHL and in civic affairs came pouring out in these conversations. I don't pretend to have captured the last word on service leadership or service sector companies in these pages. But I have been able to verbalize here my lifetime of thinking and experience about the dignity, design, and development of service enterprises and occupations in all their myriad forms. By bringing these reflections forward in *Service Reborn*, I invite you into the conversation.

Po Chung
June, 2012

A Prefacing Note from Art Bell

It is every business editor's dream to sit down, without time constraints, to engage a world-renowned business leader in a series of no-holds-barred conversations. No doubt it is every business reader's dream to read such conversations.

I was fortunate indeed to lure Po Chung into quiet restaurants, various clubs, or the Lexingford Publishing interview lounge, then close the door and "lose the key" for hours on end. Captured here are Po's unique, tested, and often revolutionary ideas on service leadership principles and strategies focused on Asia but in fact transcending locale and industry sectors.

He simultaneously offers Western business readers a clear window into Asian business thinking while offering Asian business people his insights on doing business globally. He was among the first to recognize the tectonic shift in many regions of global business from a manufacturing, product-based model to a service, process-based economy. As Po points out, the GDP of many global business hubs now stems primarily from service revenue, not manufacturing income.

The heart of Po's message, therefore, has to do with a true game-changer: understanding the service economy in all its forms, then redesigning both business and business education to make the most of that new economy. Around that core concept Po builds a support structure of associated guidelines and principles, including his original perspectives on business habitats, Personal Operating Systems, organizational DNA, dangerous "viruses" to business processes, and a host of other linked concerns. Together, these topics rise to the stature of a new vision for building service businesses, nurturing human capital, and relating with conscience to one's clientele and society.

Art Bell, PhD, Business Editor, Lexingford Publishing
June, 2012

Meet Po Chung

Po Chung is best known as Co-founder of DHL International, Asia Pacific and Chairman Emeritus of DHL Express (Hong Kong) Ltd. He was born in Macau and matriculated from St. Stephen's College, Hong Kong, in 1963. Thereafter, he attended university in the United States, earning his Bachelor of Science degree from California State University, Humboldt. He continued his education in the Stanford Executive Program in 1981 and after he retired he obtained the Master's Degree in Fine Art at the Royal Melbourne Institute of Technology (RMIT University), Australia.

Po began his professional career as Operations Manager for Topper Toys (Hong Kong), Ltd. Two years later in 1972 he co-founded DHL International Limited, the Hong Kong-based company aligned with DHL Airways Inc. of California. Under Po's and his founding partners' leadership, DHL has risen to the world's leading air express company, operating in 220 countries on five continents, employing over 275,000 people with a fleet of 12,000 vehicles and more than 200 aircraft. The company now handles more than 100 million documents, parcels, and freight annually.

DHL commits its expertise in international express, air and ocean freight, road and rail transportation, contract logistics and international mail services to its customers. Its global network offers customers superior service quality and local knowledge to satisfy their supply chain requirements.

DHL accepts its social responsibility by supporting climate protection, disaster management and education.

DHL is now part of Deutsche Post DHL. The Group generated revenue of more than 53 billion euros in 2011.

A Board Member for many prominent companies, Po also devotes enormous time to his community, region, and world. He has served in leadership roles on the Hong Kong Tourism Board, the Ocean Park Hong Kong, the Hong Kong Arts Center, the Hong Kong Trade Development Council, the Hong Kong Management Association, and the Hoover Institute (Stanford). He took leadership roles in founding and expanding the Hong Kong Logistics Development Council, the Greater Pearl River Business Council, the Centre of Asian Entrepreneurship and Business Values, and the Hong Kong Institute of Service Leadership & Management (HKI-SLAM).

In addition, Po was a long-time member of the World Wildlife Fund, several university and college Boards, and serves in high-level roles in support of the Hong Kong Government. Po served as Hong Kong's Official Delegate to World Economic Forum at Davos in 1996, 1997 and 1999. He has delivered keynote addresses to many forums of international business and government leaders.

Especially close to his heart and current day-to-day efforts are his two foundations, the Po & Helen Chung Foundation (formerly the Creativity and Education Foundation), created to promote quality education and educational reform in Hong Kong; and the Creative Initiatives Foundation, which encourages creative efforts on the part of nonprofit organizations and assists them in using proven business practices to meet the needs of their stakeholders. As a philanthropist and thought leader, Po has been a shaping influence in Hong Kong's expansion of undergraduate education in its eight major UGC-funded institutions to four years from the previous three-year system.

His many civic, academic, and business honors include Who's Who Among American Universities and Colleges, the Award of Business Excellence, Art

Patron of the Year for the Hong Kong Artist Guild, Outstanding Overseas Chinese Entrepreneur for the Republic of China, Officer of the Most Excellent Order of the British Empire (OBE), Doctor of Fine Art Honoris Causa, SBS, and Justice of the Peace. He teaches a popular graduate course on Entrepreneurship, Creativity, and Innovation at the University of Hong Kong.

In his leisure time (which he actually has, as I learned to my amazement), Po vigorously pursues his avocations as a Chinese calligrapher, a painter, a voracious reader, a classical music enthusiast, wine collector, photographer, and avid student of personal development.

Acknowledgments

My father told me that life is an entrepreneurial journey. With that vision in mind, I want to thank the following for contributing to the success, wealth, and significance of my life journey:

For helping me learn how to earn
For helping earn responsibly
For helping me share what I learned and earned with others

Family and Relatives

Helen (wife); Yana, Anca and Yangie (daughters); King Chung (brother); Wai Chung (brother); Jane Chung (sister-in-law); Pat Chung (sister-in-law); Eric Tsang (son-in-law)

Chung Choong (Father); Cheng Sook Mun (Mother); Wong Wai Chi (maternal grandmother); Cheng Siu; Yu Yuk Kit; Chung Ping Kwong; Yiu Yok Chu, Chung Po Kuen

Secondary School (St Stephen's College, Hong Kong)

Philip MacFarlane; Richard Handforth; Chien Sam; Chan Yi Tsun

Undergraduate Education (University of the Seven Seas, Whittier College, and Humboldt State University)

Marjorie Soeberg, Ruby Ivy, Frank Watson; Thomas A. Osgood; Richard Ridenhour; Richard Winnie; Diane Clare Grinsell; Mary Meier; Ken Fulgham; Ronald Fritzsche

Post Graduate Education

Stanford University Executive Program (SEP): Harold Leavitt
Institute for Advanced Studies in Leadership: Jean Lipman-Blumen
Master of Fine Art: RMIT: Terry Batt; Kevin White; Irene Barberis

Professional Relationships

Topper Toys: Alfred E. Simmons
DHL: Larry Hillblom; Adrian Dalsey; Bill Robinson; Dave Allen; Ken Sato; Bill Walden; Patrick Lupo; Paul Chan; Ho Si Man; Vivien Tsang; Henry Chan; Ernest Kwan; Toby Tse; K W Bae; Andy Tseng; Rod Feliciano; John Kerr; Jerry Hsu

Academic Professors

The Chinese University of Hong Kong: Japhlet Law
The Hong Kong Polytechnic University: Daniel Shek
City University of Hong Kong: Richard Ho
Thunderbird School of Global Management: Angel Cabrera
The University of Hong Kong: Richard Wong; Maurice Tse; Gilbert Wong; Yeung Ka Ching; Daniel Chua
University of Macau: Jacky So
Harvard University: William Overholt, Arthur Kleinman
Institute for Shipboard Education Semester at Sea: Les McCabe
Lingnan University: Chan Yuk-Shee
University of California, Irvine: David Blake, Leonard Lane
Hong Kong Baptist University: Albert Chan
The Hong Kong University of Science and Technology: Edmond Ko
Chinese International School: Ted Faunce
University of San Francisco: Arthur Bell; Dayle Smith
HKU SPACE: Lee Chack Fan

Community Service

Sir David Ford, The Honorable C. H. Tung; Anson Chan; Fanny Law; James Thompson; Alex Fong

Friends and Business

Elsie Tong; Victor Fung; Julia Fung; Malcolm Au; Vickie Au; Albert Cheng; Allen Yeung; Clara Mak; K M Wong; Saimond Ip; Shela Chan; Patrick Ho; Max Ma, John Seto; S L Chia; Lawrence Chia; Catherine Kwai; Edward Fung; Laura Cha; Godfrey Scotchbrook; Blair Singer; Choi Hak-kin; Timothy Peirson-Smith; Anthony Griffiths; Stephen Lee; Eric Wong; Ranjan Marwah; Fanny Sze, Ran Elfassy; Thomas A. Osgood.

Acknowledgments from Art Bell

The Business Editor of Lexingford Publishing gratefully acknowledges, first, the patience and consummate expertise of his interviewee, Po Chung. Working with him on this set of conversations proved not only enlightening but also a delight. I always looked forward to "coming to work."

I also thank the production staff at Lexingford Publishing for their skill in turning a manuscript into a book, a process that involves details too numerous to list but not to be overlooked. The cover design, featuring Po Chung's own graphic work, was expertly created by our long-time artistic associate, Nishant Vats.

Dedication

Po Chung dedicates this book to his dearest wife, Helen, and extends his special thanks to their daughters, Yana, Anca and Yangie.

Table of Contents

Chapter One

Service: the Business Reality of the 21st Century

Q: Po, it may be true that a journey of a thousand miles begins with a single step. But in this age of jets, we can also see the journey from 30,000 feet. Shall we begin our conversation with the "big picture" of some of your central themes? Then we can investigate each in more detail.

Sounds fine to me. But, as the politicians say, I reserve the right to come back in more detail to the topics we touch on in this overview.

Q: Po, there's an old tale of an emperor whose kingdom was under attack. He rushed to fill a jar with as many of his finest jewels as possible.

And I know how the story concludes—it has a version in almost every culture. The emperor figured out to put in his biggest gems first, then to "backfill" with as many small jewels as possible to fill the spaces in the jar.

Q: Precisely. A year from now, if readers remember nothing but four main ideas from your book, what would they be? In other words, what are your largest gems?

If I had to select my four largest jewels contained in this book, they would be as follows:

First, we ignore service to our professional and personal peril. We are surrounded by service in hundreds of forms—yet we continue to ignore the science and art of service in educating people for available careers. We must restore respect to service in all its forms, both to motivate those who will be entering service careers but also to recognize the social contributions of companies and individuals already performing service roles. We can't afford to train people for jobs that no longer exist in any significant quantity (jobs such as running factories) while closing our eyes to the millions of good jobs provided in the service sector of our economy. This is the core concept that animates all else in these pages.

Second, the server is the service. The personal character, skills, and caring of the human being providing the service determines how successful that service will be and what opportunities will grow from it. Enhancing service means nothing less than nurturing, encouraging, and developing the individual who serves. I consider these qualities, traits, and abilities to be the core "content" of service.

Third, servers do not exist in a vacuum. Instead, they occupy a place within the human habitat, along with the rest of us, and more specifically within a business habitat. The health of that habitat is all-important. No one person, thank goodness, is in charge of managing or caring for the human habitat or particular business habitats. We all play a role in ensuring that the habitat thrives and, within it, all its human residents and employees—and, in many habitats, the natural world and planet itself. Major spiritual traditions, including Confucianism, Christianity, and Buddhism, have all enriched our understanding of what makes a human and humane habitat. In a word, the habitat is the "context" of service.

Fourth, we spend our lives in large part in service to others. Once the broader boundaries and definition of "service" are grasped, we realize that we serve in dozens of ways throughout our lives. The key question involves the quality of that service, as we engage others in co-creating a mutually satisfactory service experience.

Q: Each of your main points focuses on the concept of "server." To be frank, Po, most of us don't place high status on the role of server. We think of waiters in restaurants and that sort of thing.

And that's precisely the problem: we have failed to understand the importance of service, our dependence on it, and how best to improve it. We think of service with a small "s" when in terms of its significance it deserves a capital "S." (I won't disturb the prose flow of our conversation by capitalizing "Service" each time I used it—but please consider it capitalized throughout this book.) Let me name more than a dozen servers to demonstrate the breadth of service in society. Imagine your life without them: banker, policeman, lawyer, teacher, mechanic, government clerk, parent, doctor, grocer, retailer, legislator, TV station manager, and even the fast-food delivery person.

You may never have thought of these people as servers. I could just as easily have named an array of corporate servers to show the depth of service in organizations. In a company, the owner, shareholders, board of directors, CEO, Senior Vice President, Vice President, senior managers, junior managers, supervisors, floor managers, shift supervisors, functional supervisors, location supervisors, floor and team leaders are all servers. Yet none of them "make" anything in the manufacturing sense. They don't farm. They don't mine. They don't fabricate or assemble. Their success depends entirely on the quality of service they provide to you and me. Waiters are in very good company with other servers, aren't they? Without service, the world as we know it fades to black.

Q: So please define service as you view it.

Service is any activity characterized primarily by human interaction, including interaction by electronic means, that satisfies a need. Manufacturing a widget is not service. Selling a widget is service. Growing corn is not a service. Catching fish is not a service. Flipping hamburgers is not a service. Selling that corn, fish or burger to customers is a service. I am making a distinction here, of course, between production and service.

Facebook is the great example for the younger generation, and increasingly for all of us, of service in its electronic form. There's a reason Facebook calls their main computer installations "servers," although in truth it's the people directing these electronic devices who are the real servers. Millions of people "serve" one another through the Internet, connecting on a personal and professional level to enrich their lives and fulfill their needs.

Q: People are often tempted to think of "service" as a one-way relationship, from server to the person served.

That's a narrow, outmoded view that hardly applies to the vast majority of service relationships. Service is a social enterprise by its very nature. Its value is co-created by the service provider and the person whose needs are being satisfied.

Q: Given that broader perspective, a good part of our local and global economy comes from the service sector.

Indeed it does, as does a considerable portion of any government's tax base. Let me give you a specific example. Although Hong Kong in the 1970s and 1980s gained a reputation as a manufacturing center for toys, garments, and electronics, that has all changed in the last decade. As mentioned in the Preface, at present 93 percent of Hong Kong's GDP comes from service revenue, not manufacturing. Fully 80 percent of Hong Kong employees work in service jobs in one form or another—that's four out of five people you meet every day! Driving around Hong Kong you can observe dozens upon dozens of former factory buildings that have now been converted to creative space, knowledge management locations, IT research facilities, "app" production labs, artisan lofts, and residences.

It's no overstatement to assert that Hong Kong's prosperity and well being is dependent on its government's and citizens' ability to deliver high-quality service.

And Hong Kong isn't unique in this regard. Other famous service hubs around the world include San Francisco, London, Singapore, Paris, New

York, and Tokyo. These cities are now hotspots for human interaction—i.e., service—even if they began as manufacturing centers. Sure, you can find an occasional factory or enterprise such as aquaponics and vertical farming here or there in any urban center. But by and large their populations are made up of service providers, not product fabricators (or "craftsmen," as they were once called).

The many millions of people living in these "service cities" rely on the quality (or market value) of their servers. For example, the future of my home, Hong Kong, depends on the success of the services it offers not only in its own region but to companies and individuals throughout the world.

Q: It makes sense, then, that you are concerned about the lack of attention we give to service education and training.

That's the understatement of the year! Believe me, I'm not trivializing this issue or whining that "you just can't get good service anymore." Instead, I'm arguing that we are walking backwards into the future. We are looking in the rearview mirror of history to a former age of manufacturing.

In those days you needed managers at the top who could send down orders to the rank and file, with the result that products—games, shoes, air conditioners—came tumbling off the assembly line. It was a "command and control" world in which managers needed to know how to deal with "things" more than with people. They needed typical business school courses in supply chain management, finance, accounting, information technology, and all the rest. Essentially, they needed expertise in counting and controlling.

But take a moment to look through the front windshield toward the future we are approaching. That future is increasing dominated by service professions, which operate by very different principles. Our schools and in-house corporate training programs are still teaching old-world manufacturing skills to people who will require highly developed service skills for their personal and professional success.

Product-oriented thinking is insufficient for co-creating satisfactory service relationships or carrying out the service leader's role.

Q: But let's go back to your list of service professionals for a moment. Surely you aren't claiming that doctors, lawyers, and teachers aren't receiving thorough training.

That's exactly what I am saying. Medical schools aren't spending even a small fraction of their curriculum or resources in teaching doctors how to deal well with people. Lawyers pass the bar exam knowledgeable about the law but ignorant in many ways about how to serve people with care and sincere concern. The hundreds of "lawyer jokes" make that point! As Theodore Roosevelt remarked, and John Maxwell later echoed, "People don't care how much you know until they know how much you care." (See Fiske, S. [2007] for empirical validation of this point.[1])

Teachers focus on content skills and values through their teaching, but ignore the obvious fact that their success will depend upon exciting their students about learning. Bankers focus so exclusively on their computers that they ignore the real people waiting in line for someone to handle their financial needs. In almost every service sector, employees have been ill-prepared to deal with real people and their needs. Basic skills in how to build trust and respect as the basis of professional relationships have been largely ignored in education and corporate training. In the case of Hong Kong, its education system needs to develop more service leaders and service performers by providing instruction and hands-on experience in the "people-skills" of creating trust and respect.

Q: You're saying that we're churning out people trained for a manufacturing mentality while what they actually require is a very different set of service skills.

Yes. If you don't listen attentively, people conclude that you don't care. Think about your accountant, for example. She got her MBA or other financial credential, but never learned how to listen carefully to what her clients need or want. Active listening wasn't part of the B-School curriculum.

Or pick one of your college professors at random. Did he or she know how to inspire students with a love of and thirst for knowledge—or did just the opposite occur? Did you lose whatever interest you may have had in a subject by taking a class with an extremely knowledgeable professor who never learned how to teach or demonstrate caring for his or her students?

Q: We can all think of teachers who turned us off to a subject we thought we might like. What level of service do professionals owe to their clientele?

I think it's apparent that service operates according to a "rank of sensitivity." The most sensitive service relationship—the one that requires the utmost diligence and caring—is the service relationship between parents and their offspring. That's a 24/7 service responsibility sensitive not only to the needs expressed by one's children but also to the needs they don't verbalize.

At the middle of the rank of sensitivity scale is the service commitment between leaders and those who trust them, their followers. I include in this category those who are leaders by their profession, such as physicians, professors and politicians. They obviously have less sensitivity to their clientele's needs than might a parent, but their level of caring and responsibility should be nevertheless strong.

At the lower end of the rank of sensitivity is the service owed by managers to their subordinates. I am not suggesting that no service bond exists here. Much the opposite. But in the broad spectrum of sensitivity to service needs, managers exercise a less intense and individualized form of service to their subordinates than would be required of, say, a parent or a physician.

Q: You're not letting managers off the hook for service responsibility to those they supervise, are you?

Of course not. Instead, I'm pointing out that service has degrees. It depends on the situation and context at hand. It is something we dial up and dial down according to circumstances and people in our lives. It is not a switch we flip on or off.

And those degrees of sensitivity differ in kind and quality, not mere quantity, from earlier product-oriented education and thinking. A service expert will engage in levels of reflection when faced with a problem. A product-oriented expert will consult a manual.

Q: It's hard to deny that good service seems to be low on the list for many professionals we encounter every day. Whose fault is it? Have schools let us down?

The blame game will get us nowhere. There's no one villain and certainly no single country, institution or society to point the finger at. Let me account for the problem in this general way: we have all underrated, misunderstood, and downright ignored the purpose and power of service.

We have even mislabeled service abilities in a way that makes them sound unimportant and dispensable—"soft skills," as we hear every day. Presumably they are squishy and undefined, unlike the "hard skills" of manufacturing that supposedly matter more for success. Nothing could be further from reality.

Ask your dentist, for example, whether "soft skills" matter in his practice and front office. He will probably tell you that he wouldn't have a practice without these skills—and that they were not easy to master. As one dentist told me, "Teeth don't sit down in my dentist's chair. People do—people with anxieties, pain, and problems. I focus on the person in my chair."

Q: If you don't like the phrase "soft skills" for the reasons you've suggested, what's a better phrase?

If from the beginning we had referred to service abilities as "people skills" or "process skills," I think they would have been taken with the seriousness they deserve and wouldn't be branded as "soft" in any way. After all, these are *not* the frills that decorate the edges of a service occupation. They are the heart and soul of the occupation.

I contrast "people skills" with "product skills" (otherwise known as practical or technical skills)—the latter category being the hands-on ability to craft an item of some kind. When it comes to employee learning, I estimate that it takes at least ten times the effort, expense, and engagement to teach "people skills" compared to "product skills."

It takes five minutes to teach a doctor how to administer a shot in the patient's arm. It may take days, weeks, or longer for the doctor to master the "people skills" of calming a screaming child, reassuring a skeptical parent, or coaching a medical intern.

Empathy—putting ourselves in the emotional shoes of another person—is the key here. Empathy prompts a signal to care. Do we ignore our client and belittle his concerns, or do we show sincere regard for what he is feeling? These emotions may involve pain stemming from a situation, anxieties about the future, anger over a mistake, embarrassment in front of others, discomfort in a new situation, or grief about personal and professional disappointments. In all these cases, someone who serves should give a damn—and in a way that is apparent to the client.

"People skills," including empathy, automatically motivate the desire to rise to leadership roles as needed. No one is a leader all the time in every aspect of his or her life, just as no one can completely avoid leadership at some point in ways large or small. In fact, everyone is a leader, usually more often than we tend to recognize.

Q: Let's pause there for a moment: the idea of "leadership" is often treated almost as the opposite of service skills. In many cultures, the leader is the one to be served, not to serve. The leader is the cultural or corporate king or queen.

I much prefer the notion of a leader as the ultimate service role. And it's not just my preference—it's what most leaders find themselves *actually doing*. James Kouzes and Barry Posner interviewed more than 3000 business and organization leaders at all levels to discover in an empirical way what they did on the job. Out of this monumental research came a best-selling book, *The Leadership Challenge*, which is widely used to measure and teach leadership skills in companies and business schools.

Kouzes and Posner found that leadership boiled down to five core practices: model the way, inspire a shared vision, challenge the process, empower others to act, and encourage the heart. Those sound like "people skills" to me and lie at the heart of service.

I would add three related activities that I've observed in every true leader I have worked with. First, no leader does it alone. He or she must have excellent team-building instincts and abilities. Second, no leader hides their light under a basket. Leaders are always in the process of teaching others to lead. Finally, leaders sell, sell, sell. By that, I mean that they are excited by their organization's products or services and eager to talk about it to one and all. In fact, if you aren't excited by what you have to offer, you're in the wrong business. That formula deserves highlighting: Team, Teach, Sell.

Q: You're obviously passionate about service abilities. Can you talk about the roots of that passion?

There's no one root. It's more like a root system below the ground all yielding one plant above the ground. The tap root, so to speak, was my own upbringing. My parents took their service roles very seriously. They tended to "walk the walk" and develop the "talk" later. They were people of character who demonstrated deep caring for the people in their lives, especially their children.

They taught us core values about why we serve others and how to go about it. It wasn't a matter of an occasional sermon or upbraiding. For my parents, service to others was a way of life, and it was the air that we breathed as children growing up. Although I'm sure they never wrote these attributes down, my parents focused on five goals for us as children growing up. They strove to make us accountable, responsible, respectful, resourceful, and honorable. By 'honorable,' I refer to a deeply-held code of honor. Like my parents' childraising philosophy, that code was not written down or memorized. Instead, it was lived. We almost always knew when we were keeping or breaking the code—and when in doubt we could discuss those issues with my parents.

Also on a personal note, I must share that for our entire marriage my wife Helen and I have been actively, passionately involved in building our family habitat, although we didn't call it by that word at first. She and I continue to experience the joys and challenges of parenthood, with three amazing daughters, Yana, Anca, and Yangie.

Especially in our years as new parents, we struggled like everyone else to find the balance between guiding our children and allowing them to face and solve problems on their own. My Western Classics teachers will be glad to know I didn't forget about Aristotle's model. He combined the roles of philosopher, philantrophist, and politician with one more function that probably took up most of his time: personal coach. For all his considerable wisdom, what it came down to for Aristotle day by day was what he could inspire and nurture in his pupil. How different is this insight from that of the "tiger mom" who enforces behavior through threats and punishments. And in this regard it often helped me to remember Einstein's words: "I never teach my pupils. I only attempt to provide the conditions in which they can learn." Those conditions definitely include the apprentice system—the dominant training system to this day at DHL—in which a new employee observes and emulates successful work behaviors and receives feedback on his or her progress.

Of course we didn't consider our children as our pupils. But we took Einstein's point about "conditions" seriously and tried to shape our family life so that good qualities, values and relationships emerged for all of us. I started to see the link between "bringing up" a well-trained courier for service at DHL and bringing up my daughters. While there were obvious differences, I saw that both my novice couriers and my young daughters were in search of a mentor. They wanted to learn and my wife and I wanted to teach them. The experience, in both cases, reminded me of the fine novel, *The Name of the Rose*, by Umberto Eco, in which a Benedictine monk, William, used his experience and intelligence to guide his apprentice, Adso.

In the beginning, I used the word 'environment' for this master-apprentice scenario. But that word quickly took on connotations that were too broad:

environments of clean air, clean water, and so forth. I needed a word that suggested a tighter and more manageable palette. I ended up drawing on my early days in northern California fisheries and settled on the word 'habitat'—a space with complex but interrelated variables, often beyond our knowing.

I mentioned fisheries. That was a formative and somewhat unusual experience for me and takes a couple minutes to tell. After wandering a bit in my college life, I settled on a major in Fisheries Management at a university in Northern California. You know that my main career centers around DHL, and it may seem like a long swim from fisheries to a global delivery giant. But I assure you they are deeply related.

Let me explain. As you get to know how fisheries and fish farms work, your eye is first caught by the fish themselves. It's enjoyable for almost anyone to watch them gathering for food, scrapping for the biggest bite, and at times almost flipping themselves out of the water entirely. But I soon realized that I could do nothing to care for the individual—a tiny fingerling or an especially beautiful fish, let's say—without first taking care (and I mean exquisite care!) of its habitat. In the 1960s, fish culture in North America focused on increasing the numbers of sport fish. In Asia, fish culture was akin to agriculture as a primary producer of food.

As a student I plunged into a thorough understanding of incubators, egg-taking, mating conditions, reproduction, water sampling, disease detection, nutrient cycling, tagging, estimation of population size and dozens of other topics affecting the *environment* in which the fish lived. In this way, I was extending my interest beyond the welfare of the *individual* to the welfare of the *group*. The wrong food mix in a hatchery tank, the wrong water chemistry or temperature, and you have disaster on your hands.

Maintaining a healthful habitat also includes knowing and trusting the people I worked with. They were as much a part of the total habitat as were the fish. Any one of those individuals, from the most senior scientist or professor to the newest intern, could influence the habitat for better or worse.

We all had to agree on common goals and rules for what we were doing—in effect, the "culture" of our relationships with one another and our activities. This is a long way of saying that we each bore individual responsibility for the maintenance of the habitat. If only that sense of personal commitment and caring could be extended across all business sectors!

What I carried away from these years was a profound regard for the importance of the *environment* in which people attempt to do their work. I realized that a constricting, emotionally or physically unhealthful work environment could kill the motivation of even the brightest employee. I especially learned to pay attention to the interrelations between the *individual* fish or species, the *group* in which it made its home, and the larger *universe* of the rivers, lakes, and seas, including prey and predators.

In the process of connecting the dots about what I had learned about the well being of fish with the aspirations of my future career in leadership, I recognized the enormous challenge of dealing successfully with people in all their complexity. Internally, I was relating the demands of fish farming to the more general requirements of becoming a competent leader in a service operation. To function at an optimum level at DHL or anywhere else, an employee had to have the day-to-day support of emotional well being (respect and regard from others); functional well being (solid jobs skills); moral well being (the knowledge that he would not cheat or be cheated); mental well being (tasks, training, and expectations were not overwhelming); social well being (camaraderie with others in the workplace); spiritual well being (not a particular religious creed, but instead a sense of gratifying purpose to one's life activities); health well being (care for his physical safety and health); wealth well being (the knowledge that he was moving forward, not backward, financially in relation to his needs); leadership well being (the opportunity to take on new initiatives and model the way for others); personal growth well being (the deep sense that each day is not just "jogging in place" but instead is an ongoing journey that he chooses to take); visual well being, including all aspects of one's image and appearance as a professional; and character well being, a deep and intuitive commitment to consistently doing the right things, the right way, at the right time, for the right reasons.

I know that's a long list—but take away any one element and you have the seeds for discontent and diminished performance among employees.

Therefore, as my career took shape at first as a manager for a toy company in Hong Kong and thereafter through my many years and roles at DHL, I found myself relying on insights I had developed in Humboldt State University's fish habitats and labs. It would not be an exaggeration to say I often thought of a corporation as a huge tank or eco-system in need of careful monitoring, maintenance, testing, adjustment, and occasional renovation.

The environment in which people worked had everything to do with their motivation, work habits, and specific job skills. As a company leader at DHL, I didn't think of myself so much as a boss, but rather as a *designer* and *architect* of a productive, healthful work habitat, much like the scientists and professors who taught me were architects of the fisheries they supervised. They understood (and taught me) the importance of mindful design to achieve one's goals.

Q: I've never visited a fishery in my life, but it has to be satisfying to see a habitat you've designed actually produce the results you want.

Of course. There's nothing like success to increase one's passion in business or in life generally. As I saw the developing habitat at DHL literally transform the lives of hundreds, then thousands of individual workers, I couldn't help but feel the power of service principles at work.

I'm still in awe of what these principles can produce today. I suppose this helps to explain the book created by these conversations. Frankly, I would like to turn other people on to the concepts and practices that I've found so valuable over the years.

Q: "Transforming lives" isn't a phrase we often hear in the daily grind of business. Can you think of an example?

I was a personal witness to thousands of examples. Leaving real names aside, I can tell you about an individual I'll call Ho. He came to DHL without much work experience. In his interview he impressed me as honest and hard-working, which are not uncommon Cantonese virtues. But even though he was 23, I could also see the glaze of "business boredom" in his eyes.

Although he didn't say so, I think he pictured courier work as a necessary evil to pay for his food and rent. Nevertheless, we hired him on probation to see how he would work out.

Ho's transformation began during his first day on the job. He accompanied one of our best delivery people, Chan, on his rounds. Ho's job at this point was just to observe, question, and learn. Chan really enjoyed his job and it showed. Many customers said he "brought sunshine" into their office, as corny as that might sound.

By accompanying Chan on his rounds, Ho started to glimpse a new way of thinking and feeling about the delivery business. The DHL motto at the time, "Excellence Simply Delivered," became more than just a bumper sticker to Ho. He realized that those three words summed up why he came to work and why he took pride in telling people he worked for DHL.

It wasn't all about the package for Ho; it was all about the people. He learned to treat customers as friends whom you are glad to help, not as bosses you have to obey. And having a mentor to show him the way made all the difference. Meeting or exceeding the expectations of customers brought obvious satisfaction and happiness to Chan, which Ho couldn't help but observe.

Chan's enthusiasm for the job was contagious. As Chan gradually turned over more and more responsibilities to Ho, the new employee tried to imitate Chan's best practices. The system was straight-forward: *I do, you watch; your turn to do, I watch. You do it alone, then you train others.* These men understood that DHL was not a logistics chain made up only of flight schedules and truck dispatch orders. In addition, the company depended on *links*—and the link forged between Chan and Ho, as master/apprentice—that lay at the heart of the company's endeavors and successes.

I checked in with Ho after he had been given his own courier route for a couple weeks. I could tell he was not just trying to please the boss when he told me, "I really like this job. It's hard work a lot of the time and I'm always in a rush. But seeing the people on my route is like seeing friends. They look forward to my pickup or delivery and we usually have a joke of some kind going on, or at least some friendly words. I don't tell people I'm 'just a pickup and delivery man' anymore. I say it with pride, because that's how my customers make me feel. I'm a Courier with a capital 'C.'" What was less obvious to observe but no less real was the respect and status both Chan and Ho achieved within their family lives and community. These men had self-respect for their profession, and that self-respect was contagious for those closest to them. I thought to myself, 'That's the power of the DHL *habitat*.' The surroundings provided by the company empowered these associates to think more of themselves—and, ultimately, to do more based on that new confidence.

Ho didn't just get lucky in finding friendly customers. The culture we had worked hard to design at DHL had encouraged him to act in a certain way toward customers and they responded in kind. If problems occurred on his route, we encouraged Ho not to hide these issues but instead to learn from these mistakes. We wanted him to let other people at DHL know so that they could avoid the same errors in the future.

We also gave Ho the authority to solve many problems on his own, without having to muddle through a dozen policies and triplicate forms. In effect, we were pushing decisions to the lowest level whenever possible. In a real sense, Ho didn't just represent DHL. He *was* DHL to his customers. The server was the service. DHL's philosophies of business practice became real through his actions and attitudes.

Q: But surely you also had the occasional worker who was lazy and irresponsible?

Of course. I have had to 'fire' friends over the years for shortcomings in their professional actions having nothing to do with our personal relationship. Every business has its share of problem employees, no matter how carefully you screen in the hiring process or mentor in training sessions. The habitat of a company doesn't guarantee positive results in every case. But a well-planned habitat takes a lot of pressure off the manager when a particular employee isn't working out.

Here's how: In the same way that the company habitat encourages a positive set of behaviors and values, it also punishes destructive and anti-social acts. A senior manager didn't have to "spy" to discover employees who weren't doing well. Their co-workers would tell us and others, "Hey, this guy isn't cutting it." Instead of being the enemy, top managers usually found themselves agreeing with what employees were telling them.

Q: Speaking of bad-fit employees, we need to talk about dishonesty in the workplace. It plagues almost all companies either in the form of "shrink," where merchandise disappears into an employee's purse or jacket pocket, or theft from shipments and packages.

I call this the "virus" problem. Like a physical virus, unethical behavior can spread quickly through a habitat and "kill" much of what has been achieved. It isn't "out there" floating around in the atmosphere. Instead, it resides within certain people—within what I will call their "POS"—Personal Operating System. On a rational level, employees have to weigh the short-term gains of stealing against the long-term benefit of working in a happy, ethical habitat.

Like a virus in your computer's operating system, a virus can corrupt an individual's code of personal and professional conduct—and that corruption isn't always entirely rational in nature. Now I realize that, in a few cases, a moral virus can be spawned by a sudden personal emergency, such as the need for cash because one's child needs expensive medical treatment.

But these cases are rare. Sometimes, individuals come to their new job already "infected" with some corrupt ethics. They may never have had a solid personal grounding in what it means to be an ethical person. Or perhaps they grew up in an environment or habitat where "just don't get caught!" was all they learned from parents and friends. Their "context" was spoiled—and that damage proved stronger than their knowledge of job requirements (their "content") when the chips were down. As a general rule, context wins out over content almost every time in terms of its influence on human behavior. The chain of meaning and behavior linking "context" (an employee's background) to "content" (knowledge of job requirements") to "concept" (understanding and acting on approved DHL principles) became key to the company's success.

These "bad apple" employees are those who learned early on to trust no one—and no one trusted them in return. Luckily, at DHL we had very few such employees, given the many thousands we have employed over the years. But, as you say, occasional employee dishonesty is a reality that every company has to take seriously.

Moral viruses spread quickly because unethical people exploit the trusting nature of a healthful business habitat. By a "trusting nature," I mean that a productive work environment is not designed like a police state, with elaborate shields and detectors deployed in expectation of unethical and criminal behavior.

That kind of environment communicates the message to employees, "We don't trust you and we expect you to cheat us whenever you can." Ethical people can't live and work under that kind of dark cloud. At DHL, we always assumed that we were hiring honest people. We recognized that training for character took a long time and was extraordinarily expensive. Nor could we guarantee that such training would always "take" for a given employee. Therefore, we adopted the principle of "hiring for character, training for skills." We focused on screening applicants carefully for character traits, knowing that we would be able to train them in the relatively simple skills required of a basic courier. Throughout, we reminded ourselves to think the best, not the worst, of the human race in general.

But when even a few employees fall into the trap of unethical behavior, the company environment begins to suffer and collapse. We all can recall cases where a top executive was found guilty of corruption or moral turpitude in some form. Even if others didn't imitate his behavior, the customer would despise the leader, the company, and perhaps those who worked for the company. The virus had done its damage in the eyes of the company's customers.

Trust that previously was implicit now comes under scrutiny. Do I really want to bank at an institution where a vice president stole from account holders? Do I want my name on the client list of a consultant caught up in a public scandal? Do I want to continue to buy food from a company that failed to monitor the purity of its products, allowing tainted milk powder or other dangerous goods to go to market?

Luckily, the habitat of an organization can exercise a renovating effect on many people whose Personal Operating System (POS) have been corrupted. British doctors in the 19th century sent their asthmatic patients from the pollution and fog of industrialized London to sunny Italy for a "change of environment." A similar effect can happen when a healthful habitat restores the moral fiber of its inhabitants.

Q: Following your metaphor of a virus, we all know that these germs are often impervious to the most powerful antibiotics. How can companies find the right treatment to fight the virus problem?

Well, at major airports around the world medical personnel with fever-sensing technologies try to spot ill people and quarantine them before they enter the country. By analogy, companies should follow suit. It's vital to be smart and vigilant gatekeepers from the outset. Several questions in the application form and interview should be aimed at discovering the job candidate's Personal Operating System. As we discussed earlier, from what ethical Context does the candidate come? What Content has the candidate mastered? What Concepts have become an habitual part of his or her way of doing business with others? These, taken together, help to reveal the candidate's Personal Operating System.

Just as a computer obeys a set of hard-wired or software-driven decision-making rules (DOS, OS-X, and so forth), people have inner standards, guidelines, languages and scripts that make up their Personal Operating

System in dealing with people, problems, and opportunities. Getting to know that Personal Operating System is vitally important before you sign the employment contract for a new worker.

"Yes/No" questions rarely reveal much about a person's POS. Nor does non-stop talking by the interviewer (a perennial problem across industries, where interviewers often do as much as 80 percent of the talking in a 30 minute interview.) Instead, the battery of interview questions should include several open-ended, situational questions.

For example, a candidate might be asked, "What kind of people rub you the wrong way?" or "How do you like to be managed?" If a candidate answers the first question by telling you that he can't get along with people who think they have all the answers, you have a clue about his attitude toward authority figures. If he answers the second question by telling you he likes to be left alone unless he does something wrong, that response reveals volumes about his attitude toward mentoring and coaching.

Recently, more and more companies have included an "honesty test" as part of their hiring process. In the U.S. and many other countries, the use of a polygraph (lie detector) is no longer permitted, due to unreliable results. But companies such as Integrated Management Systems have produced extremely helpful paper-and-pencil or computer-administered tests (such as their Step One Survey instrument).

Of course, these tests are better at ferreting out what a company *doesn't* want than what it does. The tests locate dishonest tendencies in such areas as a candidate's claims about past employment and salary; previous theft of money, property, data, or time; substance abuse; criminal convictions; undesirable work attitudes; and other factors influencing the hiring decision.

But what should be the virtues to which companies and their employees aspire? An extended list of any kind, like the New Year's resolutions we make, may seem overwhelmingly ambitious viewed en masse. In reflecting on the following 13 virtues, perhaps we can both pause after each one to consider its depth of meaning and breadth of application in both personal and professional contexts. Notice that the first dozen express what should not be done and the final, culminating rule suggest an overarching principle that should be obeyed. These 13 virtues harken back to Confucius and continue to serve as an excellent guide for personal and professional moral development. Each implies a "virus" or vice to be avoided in one's Personal Operating System (POS) as well as in the conduct of the company:

1. You should not be unkind
2. You should not be inappropriate
3. You should not be rude.
4. You should not be unwise.
5. You should not breach trust.
6. You should not be disloyal.
7. You should not be cowardly.
8. You should not be corrupt.
9. You should not be shameless.
10. You should not be disrespectful to the old
11. You should not be unkind to the young.
12. You should not repeat your mistakes.
13. You should forgive others.

Q: Can a person's Personal Operating System be changed over time?

Of course. Life is an entrepreneurial venture and we are each the innovators of our next hour, day, month, and year. We are all in a constant process of growth and change, hopefully for the better. In fact, a company would be ill-served if all of its employees had identical Personal Operating Systems.

Although employees should share a core set of ethical values, these workers can exhibit a healthy variety of decision-making application programs and personality types, the latter comparable to differences among laptops, desktops, iPads, and so forth. Personality appears to be deeply congenital in nature and may be very difficult to change significantly over time. But values are a different story. They are learned from experience and observation; moreover, they can be transformed by guided reflection-in and reflection-on practice. A company strives for virus-free character among its employees at all levels, and trains with the goal of developing competent, independent service operators with healthy self-esteem.

Building a strong, flexible work team often depends on choosing team members with complementary rather than identical Personal Operating Systems. Having, in effect, a variety of application programs active in employee decision-making helps to prevent a single virus from taking over the entire operating system. Some firms use personality inventories such as the popular Myers-Briggs Type Inventory (MBTI) to make sure they are not cloning the same personality type over and over in their hiring. It's not uncommon, for example, for a boss with strong planning skills to prefer only those candidates who exhibit similarly strong planning abilities (or, by analogy, the very same application programs).

But this bias backfires if it prevents the company from hiring individuals whose strengths lie in creativity, innovation, and spontaneity. As in a handful of sticks, the total strength involved in the bundle depends on whether the grain of wood in each stick is running the same direction or in opposed directions. Bundles where the grain runs the same way snap easily. Those with the grain running in opposed directions are much stronger.

Even if we value differences among people in our hiring practices, it's a different matter when a person's POS is significantly corrupted by dishonest tendencies or overly self-centered thinking and behavior. The temptation for a long-term crook to revert to unethical behavior is often too deeply engrained to overcome, no matter what the company does.

For example, a man who doesn't know how to treat women in the workplace or vice versa spells continuing and expensive trouble for any firm. If those bad behaviors are embedded in person's Personal Operating System, a company should act quickly to root out the virus. And yes, I'm talking about firing—or what's the current euphemism? "Obligatory career adjustment?"

Frankly, at DHL we were fortunate in our early years, 1969-1975, in that we only handled documents. These had value solely for the sender and consignee—there was literally nothing worth stealing in these first packages. This historical circumstance for the company helped us build a clean, healthful habitat from the beginning, as viewed from an ethical perspective.

In short, we made it a practice—one that I would recommend to all companies—to hire people who possessed character and a caring disposition. You can then train them to be competent on the level of job skills. A handy way to visualize this principle is the following formula: Quality of a Server = Skills + Character + Care.

Q: Po, we will discuss each of these issues in depth in our future conversations. But to conclude this "look out the window from 30,000 feet," is it too much to say you're calling for a revolution in the way people view their professions and are trained for them?

The word "revolution" unfortunately suggests violence, winners, and losers. I am calling for a revolution, but in the sense of the word as defined in the *Oxford English Dictionary*: "a dramatic and wide-reaching change in conditions, attitudes, or operation." Viewed as a working formula, I suggest the following: $Q = S + C^2$, that is, Q (Quality Service) = (S) Skills + C^2 (Character x Care). All elements must be present in any worthwhile educational or training program capable of truly revolutionizing service leadership and service delivery throughout the world.

Viewed in this context, no one has to "lose" in the enhancement of workplace habitats, Personal Operating Systems, or people skills. I do believe that the Service Revolution must find its place as the necessary successor to the Agricultural Revolution, the Industrial Revolution and the Information Revolution. But more about that important transition in our next conversation.

KEY POINTS

1. Service tends to be undervalued and often unrecognized as a crucial professional business sector in industrial societies.

2. Service now accounts for a large and increasing percentage of the GDP and overall employment numbers, especially in regions with declining industrial bases.

3. The server is the service. A wide variety of interpersonal skills are required to carry through a successful social interaction that fulfills the business function at hand and satisfies the customer.

4. The habitat or work environment is jointly created by all its stakeholders. The habitat sustains and promotes business activities, including the motivation of employees to perform at their best and seek to improve their job skills.

5. Service comes in many forms, including the daily activities of bankers, teachers, lawyers, mechanics, bus drivers, grocers, entertainers, and all the others who "serve" as their primary contribution to society. Not categorically involved in service are those who grow produce, mine ore, and catch food. As an operating principle, service involves social interaction aimed at satisfying a need.

6. Service can be defined as any activity primarily characterized by human interaction rather than the production of goods. Such human interaction includes contact by electronic means.

7. Schools at all levels and training organizations tend to produce graduates with a manufacturing mindset and product-oriented skillsets that are ill-suited for a modern world requiring service expertise.

8. The source of the failure to train for service skillsets is general and societal. We have not given service roles the visibility and priority they deserve. We err in labeling service skills as "soft skills," if that phrase is understood to connote a low priority of importance and lack of serious attention.

9. Company leaders are architects of the professional habitat that influences all the company is and does.

10. Well-designed habitats have the power to transform the personal and professional lives of those who inhabit them.

11. One's "POS"—Personal Operating System—is a crucial determinant of job success. Managers must guard against the presence of "viruses" in the form of moral violations that subvert the proper functioning of Personal Operating Systems in the company.

Chapter Two

Understand: The Habitat is the Habit

Q: Po, in our last conversation, you described the importance of "habitat" to any organization, including businesses. Let's start there today, and in later conversations we can discuss those who live and work within the habitat—and how to motivate and manage them.

Does it sound too much like a bumper sticker if I say, "The habitat is the habit"?

Q: Explain, please.

Let's take your professional habitat, for example. You're an editor and publisher. Certain things come naturally to you when you're at work, and you probably don't even think about them consciously. You don't let grammar or spelling errors slip by into print. You have an eye for cover design. You know instinctively what will interest your readership and what won't. You can spot good writing and bad writing.

Those are "habits" that you have developed over your professional career. Each of us has a somewhat different set of habits—but in each case they meld together to make up our individual work habitats.

As in many areas of life, we recognize when we have *left* our familiar habitat by distinct feelings of discomfort. Put a banker in the seat of a bus driver or vice versa and they will each know with certainty that they have left their "comfort zone"! To put the matter concisely, your habitat is the zone where you think and act spontaneously in ways that intuitively feel right. It's the place where you feel at home, comfortable, secure, and among friends.

Add one more thought to this proposition. Jared Diamond, in his book *Guns, Germs, and Steel*, brought back a famous sentence from Tolstoy's novel, *Anna Karenina*: "Happy families are all alike; every unhappy family is unhappy in its own way."

Applied to habitats, here's what I believe this principle means. Unsuccessful endeavors (including business ventures) can fail because they do not avoid any one of a number of destructive attributes. Endeavors succeed, however, *not* because they do one or two things well, but instead because they manage to avoid all the negative attributes that would lead to their failure. According to Diamond, a deficiency in any one of a number of factors comprising an evolving situation can doom it to failure.

The habitat of a space shuttle provides an apt example. It remains a viable environment for human life because it avoids the negative things (such as a hole pierced through its protective skin) that would doom it. All the right technologies in the world do not save a habitat that experiences a fatal flaw.

My point is that those responsible for business habitats must pay attention not just to what they are doing right, but also to the avoidance of whatever could destroy the habitat.

Q: This question may sound a bit "Zen," but do we create our habitats or do they create us?

Zen questions are among my favorites. My answer is "both." You could say that we are the "content" of a habitat, in the same way that words are the content of a book. Yet it is simultaneously true that words without a context—a book cover, title, and so forth—cease to be a book. Similarly, the habitat that is our context defines and creates us. Take away our habitat and we change, probably not for the better. All that you are, personally and professionally, goes into making up your habitat. But once established, that habitat exerts its own influence on your behavior and choices, and on those of everyone else who occupies the habitat.

For example, at your publishing company, certain things just "aren't done." I would guess that it's very bad form at Lexingford Publishing to miss a scheduled meeting with a client or show up very late for an important in-house meeting.

Where did those rules come from? At first, they came from the founders of the company and its initial employees. But my point is that the habitat *itself* begins to take over and enforce the guiding rules or culture of organization. (Note, however, that the evolution of the habitat must be carefully monitored; an incorrectly designed habitat can kill business.) When new employees come into your organization or into DHL, they "learn the ropes"—which is a way of saying that they come to understand what the habitat is all about, including its rules, goals, and boundaries—in short, learning the "code" of the company.

The code of behavior that lies at the heart of the habitat is typically not written down, but it can be. "Code," in other words, is distinct from "culture." The opening pages of many annual reports attempt this kind of written description of company "code" and in their "Mission" or "Who We Are" statements.

But underlying even these statements is a deeper, more essential code called "company culture." It is not written down—in the poet Shelley's phrase from *Prometheus Unbound*, "Deep truth is imageless." Our inability to capture "culture" with any completeness in language reflects the complexity of the subject. Try this experiment. See what answers come to mind for these questions: What does it mean to be Chinese? What does it mean to be British? We can think of the beginnings of answers, but at the same time we realize that the full answer to those questions is long and complex indeed, with much of it beyond our knowing.

Therefore, when it comes to understanding our habitats, we have to respect not only the tip of the iceberg we see (the visible, most available aspects of culture) but also the great mass that is invisible beneath the water, so to speak: the aspects of culture that influence us but cannot be formulated with any precision as bullet points in a PowerPoint presentation!

Q: My habit is to give you a follow-up question—so that must be part of my habitat as an editor! My question is this: do we just discover our personal habitats as we go through life, or can habitats be consciously created?

Let me answer that question in a business context. From my experience with major companies and many civic and social organizations, I want to emphasize that habitats don't just "happen," fresh sprung from the brow of Zeus.

Actually, let me qualify that statement: habitats should *not* just occur by happenstance or accident, even though they do in perhaps the majority of business, social, and governmental organizations. In those unfortunate cases, the so-called habitat is more of a no-man's-zone, where no one feels at home, although their names may be on the office door or the membership list.

Metaphorically, these accidental habitats are little more than a plot of land left for weeds and pests. Lacking design and intention, the habitat becomes an obstacle to thinking, feeling, and action—an environment where employees are always fighting *against* one another, themselves, and their organization.

To be true to its name, service education and the habitats it creates should place equal emphasis on teaching service competencies, strengthening character, and nurturing a caring disposition. That's the code and culture undergirding true service leadership.

Q: Again, an example of a poorly designed habitat always helps.

A good friend of mine teaches in a university which sadly has paid little or no attention to its habitat. Judged by the standards of the outside academic world, she is truly an outstanding professor, in terms of her published books, subject expertise, course innovation, and student response. She has earned international status in her field.

But internally, within the boundaries of her university habitat, administrators seem to resent all senior faculty who have risen to international prominence. These deans and other executive officers of her home university go out of their way to make it "tough" for tenured faculty, over whom they have little realistic control.

These administrators much prefer to staff their classes with junior faculty and adjuncts—untenured, poorly paid, and vulnerable at all times to termination—in order to satisfy their craving to be "bosses" in the old-style sense of "those who are to be feared." Tenured senior faculty, like the woman I've mentioned, don't fear their administrators—and therein lies the problem for these bosses.

As you can imagine, the habitat that results in this particular work environment is unproductive indeed. Those at the bottom of the salary scale come to work intimidated and dispirited, knowing that their professional fates depend on the whims of top administrators. Those at the top of the salary schedule come to work feeling they are disrespected and are being treated as little more than "dead wood" within the habitat.

Notice that in this case the habitat is the biggest obstacle to achieving the excellence and prominence sought by the university. Power is concentrated too exclusively at the top. No one wants to give their best, to try as hard as they can, in an environment of disrespect and negativity.

Q: Isn't it obvious to executives such as these administrators that their habitat has gone foul?

Sadly, no. We have all observed and probably have experienced bosses who blame everyone except themselves for organizational or "habitat" problems. In the case of the senior professors I described, their administrators meet regularly in private to bemoan the "poor morale" on the part of the faculty and their inability to hire gung-ho junior faculty.

These administrative meetings never quite "get it." The bosses at the university need to ask, 'What are we as organizational leaders doing to shape a habitat that encourages rather than discourages the best effort from all our people?' They do not understand the service nature of their university or their own roles within that organization.

Q: That raises an interesting redefinition of leadership itself. How would you define "a service leader" in an organizational habitat?

As we learned at DHL, a leader turns out to be anyone who helps to shape the service habitat in significant ways. That person may not be at the top of the salary or bonus scale. A courier, for example, who spots a problem in the way we do business, reports it to the company, and helps to find a solution is a company leader in every sense. It would not be an exaggeration to say that this person is the captain of his or her route and the master of the company's service soul.

This vision of leadership is not "top down," like the child's game "King of the Mountain." Instead, habitat leaders emerge more as what James Sipe and Don Frick call "fishnet" leaders in *Seven Pillars of Servant Leadership: Practicing the Wisdom of Leading by Serving* (2009).

Like a fishnet spread out across choppy water, any portion can be lifted by the seas and a whole matrix of connections rises with that portion. The movement of the water ("business conditions") can raise several parts of the fishnet at once, and to different heights. The image is not unlike a circus tent as it rises with its several central support poles pushing this part, then that part up higher and higher.

Leadership is much like this fishnet or circus tent image. The shape of leadership in the habitat at any particular moment depends on what the organization needs and what challenges the organization faces. As with the circus tent or fishnet, various points of leadership can rise according to the priorities of the moment. As these points of leadership rise, "subleaders" are drawn up as well, just as the network of the fishnet draws up a whole series of connected strings when one point is raised. Then, as organizational needs change, these points of leadership recede and others arise. In this way, everyone is a leader for at least 15 minutes every day. Leadership is an interchangeable practice among members of the team. Just as "form follows function" in modern architecture, so leadership follows specific needs in business practice.

Q: This is a very different idea of leadership than we're used to from our political systems and manufacturing mindset. Usually the guy at the top stays at the top as long as he can—and then is finally toppled by the next top dog.

You're right—I am describing a different view of leadership. And *viva la difference*! In a service context, leadership is aimed at ethically satisfying the needs of one's self, others, communities, and environments.

Remember that from the earliest days of the Industrial Revolution in the U.K., U.S., Europe and in Asia, those who worked in factories were fresh from rural areas. Workers had no experience with machines. In fact, one of the biggest problems in early factories was keeping workers from maiming themselves by getting clothing or limbs caught in the gears, cogs, flywheels, and other open hazards of early production machines.

In this factory environment of completely untrained, fresh-from-the-farm workers, managers took on the familiar role from English history of a liege lord or mini-king. They made the rules, dispensed rewards and punishments, and controlled virtually all decision-making.

This "top dog" world is well depicted in Shakespeare's plays. There, the great sin for an average guy was to be an "over-reacher"—one who didn't know one's "rightful place" in what A.O. Lovejoy wrote about in his book, *The Great Chain of Being: a Study in the History of an Idea*. Most of Shakespeare's villains are people who wouldn't accept their place in society, but attempted to reach for power that didn't belong to them. This idea of "staying in your place" was very much the mindset that early industrialists brought to their management of what they openly called 'the rabble.'

That approach to leadership—an isolated, all-powerful totem figure to be feared by those he privately or publicly disrespects—has carried over in our own times. *Fortune* magazine regularly perpetuates this old leadership style by its cover articles on "The Ten Toughest Bosses" in various industry sectors. Where are the magazine covers that boast about "The Ten Most Inspiring, Respected, and Trusted Bosses"?

The magazine implies that these tough individuals exemplify the kind of leadership that all organizations should have—a no-nonsense, even brutal chief who can supposedly "make the hard calls" and force their organization to "shape up." Frankly, this Mad Max approach to top leadership is organizational balderdash and business insanity.

At DHL, the "top dog" was often at the so-called bottom of the company hierarchy. We pushed decision-making authority to the lowest possible level so that every employee had the opportunity and responsibility to lead, grow, and prove themselves. This arrangement was by design, not accident: we wanted problems solved as quickly as possible by those closest to the action—that is, the couriers themselves. The last thing we wanted was to have an upset customer hear those infamous words, "That's not my department."

Q: I can tell by your tone of voice that you have major problems with top-down, authoritarian leadership style.

Was it that obvious? It is the leadership style I have tried to avoid my entire professional life. As Douglas McGregor points out, these so-called leaders basically think the worst of those who work for them—and I phrase it that way purposely.[2]

Theory X leaders see their employees as intrinsically lazy, resistant to training, incapable of original thought or action, and subversive in their plotting against the will of management. These so-called leaders really believe that all employees are clock-watchers and time-stealers, trying to do everything they can to avoid their work duties and get to the pub as soon as possible after the whistle blows or to sneak out before quitting time. These bosses also suspect their employees of low morals, and blame everything from broken equipment to missing petty cash to lost inventory on worker dishonesty.

At this point, simple self-selection takes over. There's a classic story about two young men working in a small, one-factory town. The boss treats both young men disrespectfully and lets them know that they have no option but to do his bidding for whatever he wants to pay. One of the young men decides that the risk of finding a more satisfying job elsewhere overrides any fears he might have about losing the security of the job he hates. Therefore, he packs his bag and goes off to seek his fortune and future elsewhere. Motivated by his previous bad experience, he knows what he is now looking for and he is willing to work hard for it. In a short period of time, he finds a satisfying job and rises steadily in competence and income.

The young man who stayed behind, however, sunk into a descending spiral of depression and poor work performance. His boss, in response, became more enraged than ever. One young man allowed the power of self-selection—his "quiet inner voice"—to tell him what to do and to help him find the courage to do it. The other young man heard the same inner message, but ignored it. He eventually was fired from his hated employment altogether and sank into the ranks of the ne'er-do-wells around the small town. He lost not only his job, but his self-respect and that of his family.

Needless to say, these "boss" leaders get exactly the kind of employees they deserve. Their best employees leave, and the company is left with the dregs. If workers are despised, they will often act in despicable ways. The mindset of management becomes a self-fulfilling prophecy.

At root, authoritarian leadership models undermine the ability of front-line service workers to deliver individualized personal service.

Q: But lacking strong leadership, doesn't an organizational habitat risk chaos? Doesn't someone have to drive the bus?

Someone may have to direct traffic, but that person doesn't drive all the cars. You're basically asking the age-old question, "How can the troops survive without Genghis Khan?"

That particular fear is what keeps Theory X leaders in power. The underlying notion is that the slaves must create the master, or lose all. Inspired by the oldest "hero" myths in our culture, we keep looking for the King of the Jungle to establish and maintain order, justice, and safety within the habitat.

It's King Arthur and his Knights all over again—forgetting the deeper moral of those tales: that single, centralized authority can be disastrously blind to the real nature, actions, and desires others in the kingdom--the Guineveres, Lancelots, and Merlins.

What were the last words Merlin spoke to the dying King Arthur? "Ah, Arthur, did I not warn you: Do not chase wandering fires." Too often, top corporate leaders scatter their attention everywhere except where it should be: on the health and future of their company habitat, including all those who dwell within it.

As a long line of corporate and political leaders around the world have demonstrated, an all-powerful leader can often be biased, obsessive, and blind to what's going on in the habitat around him or her. One could argue that organizational chaos emerges more often from wrong-headed Theory X leadership than from the distributed, fishnet approach to leadership we discussed earlier.

None of this is said to demonize top-down leadership. In a manufacturing context, clear orders from the top often make the enterprise run most efficiently. In a service context, however, people at every level need to build relationships with one another, with customers, and with other stakeholders. Such relationship-building does not occur simply because a directive comes down from the top.

In a balanced society made up of both manufacturing and service components, both top-down and distributed, fishnet leadership styles are necessary and appropriate. The key lies in knowing when to use which style.

Q: Help me tie together your idea of an organizational habitat with that of distributed leadership, as represented by the fishnet metaphor.

I'm struck by the fact that nature ties those ideas together for us every day, and in a thousand ways. A V-shaped flock of geese fly overhead on their way to a warmer winter climate. Which bird is the leader of the flock?

Watch them for more than a few moments and you will see the bird at the head of the V drop back from its leadership role to slide in at the back of the flock while a new, stronger bird takes leadership for a period of time.

This process of distributed leadership has been imitated in human habitats ranging from the peleton in the Tour d'France and other races to rotating team leaders in high-tech companies such as Apple to the periodic, planned passing of the power torch in city and state councils.   In this context, leaders arise accordingly to the usefulness of their particular skill sets and, having served their function, become followers to new leaders.

Or take the jungle itself, which we mentioned earlier. Except in children's storybooks, there is no "lord" supervising the incredibly complex interactions that take place in the habitat of the jungle. Instead, we observe a myriad of interactions within and among species.

The viability of this amazing network of behaviors and connections is only interrupted, in fact, by the intrusion of a source of single, central power—a bulldozer, let's say. Here I'm suggesting an analogy, of course, in the ruinous effect of "bulldozing" behavior on the part of top executives in organizational habitats.

Just as animals flee from the mechanical blade that cuts into their habitat, so men and women attuned to their work environments and customer relationships "go to ground" when they are disempowered, bullied, and belittled by know-it-all, bulldozer bosses.

Of course, I recognize that a command-and-control approach to management may sometimes be necessary, especially in military organizations and low-creativity manufacturing environments.   But even military leaders are changing their ways to involve more input from subordinates and peers.

Q: I understand how bulldozing behavior by the boss could destroy an existing organizational habitat. I can think of mergers and takeovers where the ultimate effect on the workforce was exactly as you describe. But what about in a start-up habitat? What's the role of leadership there?

That was precisely the situation in which I found myself in the early 1970s. After establishing a successful dispersed manufacturing system for a major Hong Kong toy company, I attracted the attention of a fledgling courier service, DHL, that wanted to extend its business to Asia and beyond. The timing was right: I wanted to change jobs. Adrian Dalsey, the "D" in DHL, liked the way I had orchestrated a complex network system. He liked the way I thought about people and my "can-do" mindset and experience.

Leaders of the company at that time admitted to me that they didn't pretend to know Asia and its unique challenges. They weren't asking me to "boss" anyone. Instead, they wanted me and those who helped me at the time to serve as *designers* of a habitat and *architects* of the business environment that would eventually lead to our market dominance throughout Asia. I took the job in large part because I relished the creative opportunity it presented. As was quickly apparent and very rewarding to them, I wasn't required to fit in to a top-down leadership system. I had my own ideas about how a localized service business should be structured and run.

Q: Asia is a big place with complicated cities and a daunting number of cultures. How did you begin founding the DHL presence in Asia?

A simple formula helped me at the time and continues to serve me well. I consider it the DNA of habitat development. In a business context, DNA for me stands for the Determining Nature and Actions of organizations— in short, what they *are* and what they *do*.

That DNA for companies is assembled strand by strand in the following sequence:

Understand —> Design —> Build —> Articulate —> Operate

We can talk about the specifics of each of these stages in a later conversation, but this was my orienting constellation of sorts as I ventured out onto the uncharted seas of express delivery to ever-larger regions of Asia.

Q: Agreed—we will take each stage in turn in a later chat. But for now, how does the habitat DNA you describe differ from what most entrepreneurs and intrapreneurs do?

As a professor of leadership and entrepreneurship at a premiere Asian university for most of the last decade, I've had the opportunity to observe and study many other approaches to the development of organizational habitats.

Here's what I've seen. The majority of start-ups, large and small, rush on to the "Build" stage before they really know what they want to build. It's a rueful topic of humor among Venture Capital firms that, left to their own devices, entrepreneurs will hurry out to rent buildings, buy company cars, print up company literature, and buy truckloads of office furniture—in effect, spend much of their first-round funding unwisely.

There's a reason many successful high-tech companies and other organizations started in a garage or a basement or garret (like HP, Dell and Apple). They wanted to spend their money where it mattered, not necessarily where it showed.

To prevent getting ahead of myself, I realized that a lot of *think-time* or understanding was necessary before I could ask the parent company to spend money in particular directions. That think-time was largely devoted to the key issue of what organizational habitat we needed to build in Asia, or anywhere else for that matter. I focused on how to organize and operate a network that is not linear and close-minded, like a manufacturing business, but instead is "open-minded" to new information that pours in every day. I understood how important relationships were to the success of DHL in Asia, and what it took to build and maintain those relationships.

No matter what local business habitats DHL had developed in the U.S. or Europe, the question I had to ask was what kind of habitat would be uniquely suited to the untested regions of Asia. That was the "Understanding" part of my work.

Q: Understanding what, specifically?

A cornucopia of issues, but let me give you some items. To say the least, Asian cities are not laid out in a grid of any kind. Addresses, road names, available parking, and different languages make pick up and delivery of anything a huge challenge, much less delivery of documents and packages that are time-sensitive.

So the first reality I had to face was that I needed a network of "local experts" (my way of thinking of my couriers and local partners) with a high degree of local knowledge instead of a corps of bosses who had never walked the streets of Bangkok, Ho Chi Minh City, or Tokyo. In the latter case, addresses don't typically go by road or number. I can't overestimate how valuable such local knowledge on the part of my first hires proved to be for the quick growth and eventual market dominance of DHL in Asia.

If a Mom and Pop auto-body shop in Zhuhai needed a crucial Honda part, my guy on that route needed to know how to get to the shop most efficiently in the light of traffic conditions and all his other deliveries, how much latitude he had to double-park if necessary for a few minutes (knowing the local police often helped!), and who in the shop could legitimately sign for the package.

As important as the timely delivery itself was, I wanted the customer to think of the DHL delivery person as "his" guy, not mine or the company's. The DHL delivery person became a necessary and dependable extension of his enterprise.

My other experts "on the ground" were DHL's customers. They knew that part of our regular training and mantra for couriers was to remind them of the importance of the documents and other packages they picked up and delivered for customers. Any delay would cost these clients both money and business. And who better to reinforce our words than the clients themselves? We invited them to speak to our new recruits—in effect, to do the "show and tell" for us about the importance of timely, reliable courier service. Nothing could have made a stronger or more lasting impression on our growing team.

In short, DHL helped its clients to be more competitive by partnering with them and co-creating value in their enterprise. This idea of partnership—everywhere in today's business—was a radical idea in the early 1970s. At that time, the post office and airlines were perceived by clients as obstacles to their smooth, profitable operations rather than as helpers. Air freight forwarders and customs brokers had the same reputation, from the client's point of view: agents of red tape, unnecessary delays, and government bureaucracy.

Meeting the goal of being a partner to our clients involved building a relationship. It goes without saying that different cultures build good relationships in very different ways. In Thailand, for example, a delivery person typically would show a high degree of deference to the customer and would display the customary "prayer" gesture of the hands accompanied by a slight bow.

That same behavior would backfire entirely among the more blunt Cantonese in my hometown of Hong Kong. There a brief, pleasant greeting and perhaps a quick but sincere show of interest in some aspect of the customer's business (in the case of the auto shop, maybe a car being worked on) would be more natural and successful in moving the relationship forward.

These local-knowledge experts dressed in DHL uniforms also became my best feeder system for finding new employees as the organization grew. In many cases, they had grown up with the people they recommended for positions with DHL. They knew who had good work habits and who was a flake. They also knew these people's track record of ethics—a crucial issue for DHL, in that its packages could contain everything from irreplaceable documents to credit cards.

Not to harp on metaphor again, but this was the "fishnet" of on-the-ground leadership that I had to understand from the beginning. The most meaningful contributions would come from within the habitat, not "top down" from any executive suite. In fact, we had no executive suites until much later in the company's evolution in Asia.

I also had to understand from the beginning that my customers were under their own pressure to send out or receive DHL packages on time. We absolutely had to deliver papers to, let's say, a real estate agent in Shanghai on time. This meant picking the documents up on time as well, or accommodating the special needs of sending customers whose documents weren't ready by the scheduled time of pickup. If our couriers weren't able to make decisions on their own, on the spot, then we might set off a chain reaction of disappointment not only for him or her but also for the buyers, sellers, financers, insurance agents, and others involved in the signing of the deal. This realization involved "systems thinking" for us all. We were nurturing and caring for a habitat, not obeying some external set of rules.

We had to adjust when the habitat was under stress. Solutions had to be prompt and reliable. Like the systematic care of fish in a tank, pond, or lake, we needed to be vigilant about our clients' needs and innovative in our thinking. Usually we had no time to wait for "top-down" decisions. Fish have a way of dying in the meantime!

In a real sense, I had to come to grips with the reality that DHL was not a "three strikes and you're out" company. We had one strike at most to please our customers. Frankly, this reality was an adjustment for me, coming from the toy industry. Although we always attempted to deliver shipments of toys on time, the roof didn't cave in if we experienced a delay of a day or two. At DHL, we rarely had to deal with a second or third strike situation because we cared about the clients' wellbeing and had professional pride in our ability to deliver as promised. Three strikes on the same mistake was simply not acceptable to anyone at DHL, least of all to the couriers themselves. It violated the rule and spirit of the habitat.

I knew that latitude wasn't going to be the case with DHL. The habitat we eventually designed or modified quickly needed the good vibes of friendly relationships with customers but also a tight rein on the quality of our service. We couldn't let familiarity breed contempt.

On the contrary, we wanted familiarity with our clients to breed understanding and compassion! I had to sell the merits of the company by putting myself in their world and understanding their needs, as different as they might have been from client's needs in New York City or even parts of Hong Kong. I wanted to encourage a culture of caring within each new locale we served.

We often found that in entering a new regional or political environment (a new "habitat"), the low key approach was best. We operated "under the radar" (but not outside the law) to introduce ourselves to the airlines and customs officers as a way of educating them to what we do and to build trust. Couriers often took the lead in building these relationships, further pleasing ("enchanting" would not be too strong a term) the customer.

Q: I assume that the "Understanding" piece of the habitat DNA you describe was an on-going activity.

Of course. The key lay in our constant attention to listening to our customers' needs. The Understanding piece was one of those crucial activities. Many times we thought we understood a particular market or a new sector of clientele only to be surprised the next day that we had missed important business or cultural features.

The phrase "think globally, act locally" (which we coined in the early 1970s and should have copyrighted!) was applied to every town, village, and neighborhood we served. Our mindset was to build a true network, not to focus only on the high-rise business towers of Hong Kong, Beijing, and Shanghai. Holding fast to this mindset, we transformed the culture of DHL to a company that took risks in serving areas previously locked out of efficient courier service. Our attention to the local aspect of our business proved crucial to our success. We took on the challenge of reaching beyond the low-hanging fruit.

And there were arguments along the way, as in any family. For example, MBAs in the company wanted to use the word "customer" universally. However, I liked the word "client" because it seemed to fit better not only with the people we were serving but also had the effect of upgrading the attitudes and behaviors of our couriers. A similar disagreement came up with regard to calling what we did a "service" or a "product/service." Favoring Occam's razor, I opted for the simpler, more elegant statement of "service." And, inevitably, you win some and you lose some of these arguments. I won on the "services" term and they won on the "customer" verbiage.

Q: And I assume, further, that habitats varied widely as you opened new markets throughout Asia? It must have been a challenge to understand the diversity of the regions you were preparing to serve.

We were reaching far "outside the box" on many occasions. But we had to keep remembering what we *did* have to offer our clientele, not what we didn't. We just had to think creatively about all the ways in which that advantage could be used. And I admit, we sometimes reached understanding through trial and error as well as acting on our intuitions and insights. But it was helpful to us from the beginning to distinguish between the master habitat—that being the overall environment of the company—and sub-habitats that emerged within that extended network.

Q: You're saying that a company has to "read" its region carefully to determine what kind of business habitat to establish?

Absolutely. And much of that "reading" process—I'll call it "sensing"—is done at the grassroots level of the company, not in the executive suite. By the time the news appears in the *Financial Times*, the opportunity may already have slipped through your fingers.

At DHL, for example, the chances are good that a courier will be among the first to hear about a potential new client preparing to lease a building or open a new shop. That information is vital if our marketing people are to have a first-mover advantage to do their jobs selling the new client on

DHL services. Therefore, in our overall company habitats and its various sub-habitats, we encouraged and rewarded the upward flow of information.

This communication direction reversed the direction we observed in so many other companies. There, information—especially directions and commands—flowed downward from the top bosses to the rank and file. In authoritarian companies, workers quickly got the idea that management wanted them to "park their brains at the curb" when they came to work, since their observations, intuitions, insights, suggestions, and problem-solving ideas were not welcome.

Mind you, no company executive exactly said those words. But the *construction of the habitat* in those firms made upward communication from employees very awkward, if not almost impossible. A good idea germinating at a lower echelon of the company organizational chart usually withered on the vine. It had nowhere to go.

We resolved at DHL not simply to hope for upward communication but to put in place actual channels by which every member of our company team at all levels could provide valuable input on how we could all do our part to make our business better.

Q: Let's turn the corner now to a special form of habitat you mentioned earlier—the service-oriented habitat. What is unique or special in the DNA of the service habitat?

Much more than in any business environment I can think of, the service habitat depends for its survival and success on a particular skill set and personal attributes of its people. You see, in a product-oriented habitat, you can have workers with a wide array of personalities and social abilities. If Zhan is putting together computer boards in Shenzhen, it isn't crucial to the business whether he is an extrovert or an introvert, just so he gets his job done well.

But in a service habitat, every representative of the company who contacts the public must have at least three main skill sets active and in balance at all times. These are, first, the ability to make people feel good in your presence and, in turn, for you to feel good in their presence.

This item may seem like a Sunday School lesson, but it turns out to be crucial for quality service at all levels. By the verbal and non-verbal signals we send (including eye contact, facial expressions, signs of interest, and so forth) we let people know loud and clear whether they matter to us or whether they are just obstacles we need to get past. Positive signals of personal engagement for service people include a pleasant, sincere smile; making eye contact during an appropriate word of greeting or expression of interest in the other person; patience if the other person is busy at the moment we want their attention; and courtesy to those associated with the main person we're dealing with.

Here I have in mind the countless service people who act in a friendly manner to the main person in an office, but show negligence and negativity to that person's secretaries and other staff. There's wisdom in the old saying that you can judge a new business associate by how he or she treats the waiter at lunch. Productive social relationships are dependent on each party possessing valued character traits and a caring disposition toward the other.

Second, the service representative has to respect the other person's time. This requirement may seem to contradict the notion of showing friendliness, but in fact they go together in balance. Business can't get done if every service call (no matter what the industry) turns into a time-consuming "gab-fest."

The service representative needs to communicate that he or she knows how busy the client is and will therefore take care of business as efficiently as possible—but not, as I've said, without the gestures of friendliness that build good relationships.

Finally, the service person must be an on-the-spot problem-solver. The idea of lower-level employees solving problems is relatively new in the history of

Eastern and Western business. The factories of the Industrial Revolution had little room for employees "tinkering" with machines and certainly no room for their comments or contacts with clients.

A person running a knitting machine in mid-19th century London, for example, wasn't supposed to sketch out a new sweater design to show to a client or figure out a better way to attach buttons. Laboring away at the machine, he or she was expected simply to "do the job".[3]

Successful service people, on the other hand, consider that part of "their job" is resolving any issues or problems they can reasonably handle. This movement toward immediate employee involvement in dealing immediately and personally with client problems showed up in a widely-publicized decision by Scandinavian Airlines (SAS) in the 1970s to empower flight attendants and gate agents to resolve a wide variety of customer problems, including requests to switch seats, have special meals, or get assistance stowing their luggage. The goal is to make the customer's problem your own. In a business sense, it really is!

While these matters may seem trivial today, at the time they were greeted with amazement and gratitude by the flying public, who had grown used to flight attendants operating by the specific terms of their union job agreements, not according to customer needs.

Q: But when you give service people extra responsibilities to deal with customers, don't they feel like you're asking them to do extra work?

In my experience, employees like to be treated as the intelligent, resourceful people they are. They don't want to be told just to do the most basic aspects of their job and not to exercise their creativity and problem-solving.

I'll give you an example. Phan, one of our delivery people in Vietnam, heard one of his customers complaining about the danger of having small delivery packages snatched off his busy work counter by customers walking in and out of his shop. Instead of shrugging his shoulders and thinking "that's your problem," Phan took a few minutes to sit down with the customer to figure out what the two of them called a Secure Box where smaller DHL packages could be safely left.

It was a simple but practical solution. The client was happy and Phan had the satisfaction of "going beyond the call of duty" in resolving a customer issue. Together, they co-created the service that made DHL a valued asset to the client's business.

Some recent scholars have differentiated "machine companies" from "innovative" or "diversified" companies.[4] In these latter forms of business organization, the *last* thing a good manager wants to do is to shut down the problem-solving capacities of his or her employees. At DHL, we built cultural norms into our habitat so that the client didn't think of a DHL courier as a "guy with a bag or package," but instead as a person with business and logical logistics solutions.

Q: Your description of company organization is reminding me more and more of a sports team. The real action is carried out by the heroes on the field— supported, of course, by the coaches and trainers on the sidelines.

That analogy almost works for me. Surely at the top or "coach's" level, the core philosophy, strategies, and tactics of the company were decided. The coach managed the well being of his players. But here's the glitch in the sports analogy: we were playing in the courier service sector while its basic rules were still in a state of flux. It was as if we were on the playing field at the same time that we were coaching from the sidelines. For example, in our efforts to serve our customers we often encountered external regulations that made no sense. Instead of attempting to build a business on the basis of those rules, we strategized to rewrite them. We changed the postal monopoly. We worked with the airlines to revise many of their rules. We even had success getting customs to modernize and streamline their procedures.

But the players on the field were still our couriers. In a very real sense, I personally cannot delight DHL customers by the quality of our service.

Only our people "on the ground" can do that. So, as a coach of sorts, it becomes my role to reinforce goals and guiding principles, run "training camps," and watch "game films" (that is, pay attention to the actual performance of employees) so that I can help them achieve incredible results. Above all, the coach encourages each player to rise to a position of leadership when circumstances call for it.

KEY POINTS

1. The habitat is the habit. This statement means that our personal and professional habitats incorporate the sum total of our cultural backgrounds, principles of behavior, standards of judgment, and conscious and unconscious beliefs and assumptions. What we do "by habit" is the best indicator of what in fact is our habitat for work or life.

2. Habitats are created by us, but they also act to create us. Once established, habitats have an influence on our choices, perspectives, behaviors, interactions with others, and ways of doing business.

3. Habitats don't just "happen." They can be purposefully and consciously created around a desired set of values and professional attributes.

4. Company executives are often the last to recognize when a work habitat is failing. Sometimes these executives are too defensive to admit that their work in building a particular habitat has not been successful. At other times, executives fail to listen to the inhabitants of the habitat—the men and women throughout the organization who could tell "the boss" what was happening to the habitat, if he or she would only listen.

5. True leaders within an organization are those who influence the habitat for the better. These individuals can be found across the entire spectrum of the organizational chart, not necessarily at the top.

6. Distributed leadership in an organization can be viewed as a "fishnet," where any section can be raised to temporary prominence, and with it the matrix of supporting functions required by that leadership. Several points of leadership can be raised in this way to different "heights" of importance, depending on organizational needs.

7. Every organization has a distinguishing "DNA"—Determining Nature and Actions—that dictates (often unconsciously) the choices made by that organization.

8. The elements of an organization's DNA consist of Understanding, Design, Building, Articulation, Operation.

9. Because valuable business expertise can exist at all levels of the company hierarchy, channels must be put in place and nurtured so that this expertise can be tapped as an input for company decision-making.

10. Companies who value their professional habitats put a variety of "sensing" mechanisms in place that capture the intuitions and insights of employees at all levels of the organization to allow for upward communication of valuable information.

11. The DNA of service-based habitats expresses itself as: a) sensitivity to people and their differences; b) respect for the client's time and need for efficiency; and c) problem-solving skills, so that obstacles to performance can be resolved on the spot.

Chapter Three

Design: the Architecture of Success

Q: Po, in 2007 you published your well-received book, The First 10 Yards: the 5 Dynamics of Entrepreneurship. How would you relate that work to our present conversation about the service sector?

The short answer is that this present book builds upon and extends my earlier work. Both are about the initiative, knowledge, and skills involved in bringing business ventures to success. In *Service Reborn,* I focus specifically on the huge service sector in virtually all developed economies. In the same way that *The First 10 Yards* demonstrated five related dimensions of entrepreneurship, here I follow a process-oriented approach to describe the primary components of what we have already discussed as the "DNA" of service: Understand, Design, Build, Articulate, and Operate.

I've chosen to investigate the service sector in this book not only because I know it best, having spent the majority of my working life (so far!) in DHL, the ultimate service company, but also because the service sector is largely unexplored territory in business and management literature as well as in business classrooms. Most of our theories about business development and management spring from the context of manufacturing, including its aspects of supply chain management, IT controls, levels of command-and-control leadership, principles for quality control, strategies for marketing, management styles, decision-making skills, and so forth.

Frankly, that's a very different "curriculum" from the core topics required for success in the service sector—a portion of the business world, we must remind ourselves, that is already predominant in most major urban centers and growing exponentially faster than the manufacturing base of a former age. After all, the world of manufacturing has a built-in linear model for creation of the end product, as can be seen in the typical production line.

By contrast, the world of service has a holistic, culture- and relationship-influenced process by which it evolves each day. Unlike finished products on a shelf, the end results of services are re-enacted anew every day, and never in precisely the same way with different people. In this sense, service has no shelf life. It is either fresh or nonexistent.

The 2007 book relates to the present work especially in its theme of entrepreneurship. Even if we have not started an enterprise or been called an entrepreneur by others, in truth we are each voyagers on an entrepreneurial sea.

Our entire existence—made up of unique experiences never lived exactly this way by any of the billions of people before us or now alive—can rightly be viewed as the biggest entrepreneurial venture in which we will ever be involved. I tell my students, "Life is an entrepreneurial journey, and you are the entrepreneur of your life."

Those words are simultaneously full of hope, in that they describe life as an adventure always unfolding, yet also full of awesome responsibility: we are the captains of our own fates, as Tennyson reminds us, and like any captain we bear responsibility not only for our own welfare but also for those we "bring aboard" in terms of our associations and influence.

Service involves its own special brand of entrepreneurship. In giving and receiving services (paid or unpaid, financially rewarded or psychically rewarded), we "take a journey" that involves commitment to others (and therefore the requirement of a high moral code or well-honed "personal operating system" on our part), new discoveries involve all our senses, especially our listening powers and intuition, and provide opportunities for quantum personal growth (measuring our courage and love of life) and increasing our capacity to serve.

Q: How does the service sector make use of a person's entrepreneurial ambitions and abilities?

In many ways, service is the crucible of entrepreneurship. In service relationships with others, we put into practice the core dynamics of the entrepreneurial process itself. Those dynamics, related to but extending on my 2007 book, focus on who, what, who else, where, and how.

In a service context, "who" refers to the doer or operator of the service. What can be said about this individual? What qualifications and skills should he or she bring to the service relationship? What "personal operating system" encourages trust and discourages malevolence? Many of these matters are not technical in nature, but instead spring from the server's deepest personal and moral nature: "the server is the service," in the sense that trust, reliability, confidentiality, and other human qualities are primary determinants of how successful the service proves to be.

Bear in mind that the person being served plays a crucial role in co-creating the value of the service relationship. That person, empowered and encouraged by a good relationship with the server, makes his or her needs known so they can be satisfactorily addressed. Moreover, the person being served can be an invaluable source of specific information about the quality of the service being provided. Viewed in this way, a satisfying service transaction involves both parties, linked by their positive relationship, in creating the service experience they both desire.

The "what" refers to the nature of the service at hand. How can that service be described in its most efficient, effective form? What human needs are satisfied by the successful fulfillment of such service?

The "who else" points to the team and the customer who help you perform your service as well as to your many suppliers and other stakeholders in your enterprise. This is a key difference between the 5 Dynamics of Entrepreneurship and service leadership.

The "where" refers to environmental contexts—both the habitat from which the server comes as well as the habitat he or she enters to perform service. These contexts can include external agents such as regulators and government process who influence the service process.

Finally, the "how" describes the tools and skills necessary to optimize the service relationship. Companies typically provide training in the use of these tools and the application of these skills as part of an employee's orientation and, through on-the-job learning, as part of his or her on-going mastery of the job. DHL added the skill of contributing to the improvement of the habitat.

Q: You have described service as a crucible or test of moral qualities, not just technical skills. Please clarify.

Let me use a simple analogy. You hire me to key in a page of your words and print them out. That's a technical act that does not draw deeply or essentially on who I am as a person. It simply requires that I have a modicum of keyboarding and printer skills.

But change that scenario slightly: you hire me to act as your negotiator in selling your printed words to a publisher. Now I find myself in a service role, as your "agent," that requires more than technical skill. In representing you, I must draw upon my own moral base or "personal operating system" to practice virtue and avoid vice. By that, I mean that I must conscientiously seek your best interest in striking a "deal" with the publisher while avoiding the selfish temptation to take whatever the publisher offers in a wrong-headed effort to "get my cut" at your expense.

Service, in the case of a DHL courier, is not merely the technical act of picking up an important package or handing it to the client. In this case, the client is relying on a wide range of moral virtues in the courier to ensure that the service relationship is successful.

For example, the recipient trusts that the courier will not steal from the package (and, yes, DHL does ship diamonds). The recipient relies on the courier's good-faith effort to "pull out all the stops" in endeavoring to the get the package delivered on time—a professional commitment the courier takes on when he or she dons the DHL uniform.

Finally, the recipient relies on the courier's utter respect for privacy and confidentiality. Extremely sensitive documents are delivered by DHL, including divorce negotiations, proprietary patent applications, highly sensitive personnel matters, and top security stock and bond information. In all these areas, "the server is the service" precisely because his or her *whole person* is committed to the successful service relationship.

The old Irish joke goes that, in a ham and egg breakfast, the chicken is involved but the pig is committed. Surely in any meaningful service relationship the server is not only involved but committed.

Q: There's a noticeable urgency about your passion for discussing service, Po, that seems to transcend usual academic interest. Why do you care so much about it?

Here are three quick but deeply considered answers to that question. First, I care because I have spent my life in service and, more particularly, in service leadership roles. I feel an obligation to share what I have learned.

Second, I recognize that my own region, Hong Kong, is dominated by service providers. Frankly, the future of Hong Kong and cities like it around the world hangs in the balance of whether these services are successful. Other regions can obviously out-produce us. Our future rests on out-serving our competition and the ability to motivate manufacturing economies to rely on Hong Kong's service expertise, character, and care.

Finally, service is a spiritual calling not in a narrow religious sense but in the broadest context. As John Donne reminds us, no one of us is an island with only our own needs to consider. We are joined in a complex and often wonderful network with other human beings—a network often characterized by service relationships in various forms. I want people to understand those service relationships more deeply so that they can find more joy in giving and receiving them.

Q: Words like "joy" and "spiritual" are relatively rare in business discussions. You have taught and presented at some of the world's top "hard-core" business schools. What response do you receive when you describe this broader spiritual context?

First, I make clear that I am not out to convert anyone to anything. By showing how three Eastern spiritual traditions may play into the development of whole, happy people serving in an ethical business environment, I am "filling in the gaps" for many Western students and business people who have grown up exclusively in a Judeo-Christian environment.

I do so in the same spirit that the renowned economist and sociologist Max Weber wrote and taught his most famous work, "The Protestant Work Ethic and the Spirit of Capitalism" (1904). With Weber, I am convinced that deep and often unspoken assumptions and beliefs about ourselves and others underpin our actions and intentions in personal and business life. You can call these assumptions "spiritual" or "philosophical." The point is that they are profoundly influential on what we do and who were are.

My relatively succinct mention of Buddhism, Confucianism, and Taoism is a modest effort to help "East meet West." We all have much to learn from one another, and from one another's traditions. I find that business students in Western nations know very little about Eastern spiritual traditions.

If anything, they conceive of Eastern religions as exclusively a matter of self-deprivation, long periods of meditation, and an absence of hair! By the same token, Asian students have little background in Western theologies and ethical philosophies. As a "global village," there's work to be done in sharing what the 19th century critic and poet Matthew Arnold called "the best thoughts of the best minds."

Q: This is an impossibly large question, but what do Buddhism, Confucianism, and Taoism have to offer a Western audience, especially those involved in or contemplating service-oriented careers?

Large questions are often the most enjoyable. Here's a short answer. We would all no doubt agree that we each inhabit and experience three worlds every day. First, there is the world of the self, with its internal concerns about hunger, security, health, ambitions, inadequacies, and so forth.

Second, there is the world of others—those with whom we are close, those with whom we are merely acquainted, and those who we know to be "out there" but have never met. Finally, there is the world of systems and machines—our cars, our governmental regulations, our transportation system, our economic system, and all the rest—the "dynamo" referred to in Henry Adam's epic essay, "The Dynamo and the Virgin" (1900).

If you consider a spiritual master, dead or alive, to be a "life coach" of sorts, the Buddha is revered by countless millions as a counselor to the first world, the inner self. Buddhism in its various forms teaches ways to focus the mind, find inner peace, recognize and avoid vice, and quiet the emotional storms that rage at various points in all of our lives.

Confucius speaks to the second world, that made up of all the "others" in our lives. He teaches virtues that encourage positive, productive relationships with others and discourage needless conflict.

Finally, Taoism addresses the "big picture" of systems of all kinds in which we find ourselves enmeshed—including the biggest systems of all, the global environment and the universe itself. Taoism offers ways to think about and cope with these systems so that the individual does not get lost among the stars, so to speak.[5]

My hope is that out of this wealth of reading suggested in the Resources portion of this book will come deeper insight into the "why" behind the busy-ness that makes up our professional lives and is often in danger of taking over our personal lives.

Q: Do Western students and business people find useful insight in what you suggest about the Buddhism, Confucianism, and Taoism?

What others find or don't find useful is entirely personal and unpredictable. Like any spiritual exploration, the destination is unknown from the outset. My purpose is simply to remind readers that these paths are available, have been well-trodden over the centuries, and may be of value to them.

The Buddha had a good sense of humor about such things. The legend goes that, after meditating with minimal sustenance under the Bodhi tree for 49 days, the Buddha attained enlightenment. When asked by his disciples what that moment was like, he responded "Not much."

Anything of a spiritual nature that I refer to here is in that same vein: perspectives on living and working that, once grasped, are seen as natural and expected in the order of things rather than as exotic or parochial—in short, "not much."

Q: Our conversation today focuses on design, perhaps the most creative stage in the development of any business. What sources of knowledge or inspiration do you draw on in the design stage of any one of your many business ventures, particularly in the service sector?

Although I am technically trained by my early education and university experience which included a healthy dose of general education, I am also liberally imaginative due to my later degrees, personal reading, painting, musical interests, and other avocations. I find that I draw on this liberal side of my self-education as much as I rely on my technical business knowledge when entering the Design stage of any business development.

Q: You have been a trail-blazer in your own professional life, including your many civic endeavors and leadership roles. Speak a bit about what drives you to find an original path—Robert Frost's "road less traveled by."

Originality is simultaneously a strategy for self-fulfillment and for business success. As Kim and Mauborgne have argued brilliantly, using conventional thinking to position your company in the same "space" as all your competitors is a recipe for failure. It means you're swimming in the "red water," where companies and people are eaten alive—"Nature red in tooth and claw," as Tennyson wrote.

To escape those waters, a person working on the Design phase of any enterprise has to think "outside the box." As familiar as that phrase has become, it's still hard to do. Thinking outside the box often requires that we turn out backs on conventional wisdom, including the lessons of some of our most admired and famous teachers. We have to use our imagination, that mysterious force "where sacred rivers run," in Coleridge's phrase.[6]

The headwaters of the imagination within each of us include dozens of influences, experiences, and forces. These range from novels and poetry we've read to music we have enjoyed to hikes and travel and art museums—all the "freeing" activities that allow our minds to wander and play, to speculate and wonder. It's in that realm where inspired Design is born.

The payoff is that, once we free ourselves to think broadly, mindfully, and originally about Design issues, we discover we're in "blue ocean" waters with few dangers around us and untapped resources to pursue.

Q: We have agreed to call this chapter "Design: the Architecture of Success." My image of business people usually involves them running an enterprise, or simply running around. I seldom picture them in a thoughtful, reflective "design" role.

I think it was a general manager of the Brooklyn Dodgers who said, "Luck is the residue of design."[7] When we see successful companies heralded on the covers of business magazines, we have a temptation to tell ourselves they were just "at the right place at the right time." It's more likely that they found and used the right design for their enterprise.

We have all heard the expression "going off half-cocked." It refers to the mistake of young, inexperienced soldiers in the American Revolutionary War rushing enthusiastically into battle without properly preparing their musket to fire. That's unfortunately the situation with too many businesses in their initial stages. They rush ahead in an effort to "do" before they think about who and what they "are" or aspire to be.

"Design" is just a single-word way of saying intelligent, creative blue-printing of what you intend to build. It is model-building in the purest sense—and better that business mistakes should be discovered at the model stage than after the business has made its public debut!

I have always admired what Jerry Porras wrote about the importance of design for personal accomplishment. It's easy to apply his words to design thinking for organizations as well as individuals:

"By embracing a thoughtfully designed, deliberate practice, you can make yourself into any number of possibilities—you can even make yourself great. Once you are clear on what you are deeply passionate about, talent has little or nothing to do with greatness. On the other hand, work has everything to do with it. In this very real sense, talent is built and not born." [8]

Q: Po, we've talked already about the importance of a "habitat" for business success. Let's talk about how one goes about designing such a habitat.

That's a huge question, of course, that many business gurus have devoted their lives to. If I had to recommend a crash course in such authors, I would especially recommend Yuan and Meiru's *Anatomy of the Chinese Business Mind*, Morgan's *Images of Organizations*, Drucker's *The Effective Executive*, O'Toole's *Good Business*, Kotler's *Principles of Marketing*, Armstrong's *The Essential HR Handbook*, and Ross's *Fundamentals of Corporate Finance*.[9]

I don't want to re-invent the wheel or venture unnecessarily into dangerous "red waters" of traditional thinking by talking at great length about the many established ways to design business habitats. Instead, let me exercise my imagination and yours for a few minutes to bring something new to the issue of design.

I'll discuss two aspects of design that are seldom discussed and even less frequently put into practice. First, I want to focus on the initial stage of building a habitat. I'll call that first stage the "locus," Latin for the "place." Then I'll talk briefly about designing the architecture of human motivation, with particular emphasis on the service sector.

Fair warning, however: along the way on these topics we'll be reaching far beyond the usual concepts and cases of business. Imagination has no required boundaries.

Q: Challenge accepted! Let's board the magic carpet to understand what design is all about.

In Michelangelo's famous fresco in the Sistine Chapel, Jehovah's finger reaches out to spark life by touching the extended finger of Adam. This touch is the *locus*, the place where the action is, the divine ignition that passes between them. In another locus moment, consider Alexander Graham Bell in his workshop in 1876 transmitting those crackly words by telephone, "Mr. Watson, come here. I want to see you"—the birth of the Media Era.

Similarly, any business habitat has its locus—and that place of beginning, that spark, can vary widely from organization to organization. For a service business (and we have already discussed how wide an occupational and professional swatch we mean by that term) the locus is not a meeting with a venture capitalist or a business plan or the printing of company stationery or the renting of commercial space.

Instead, the locus of the habitat of any service company is authentic contact with the intended customer. By contact, I do not mean a review of demographic pie charts or the reading of focus group transcripts, as valuable as these may be at some stage.

Contact means standing in the workplace of your target customer and listening, probing, and empathizing until you know his or her business needs intimately. That's the locus, the spark, that gives birth and shape to the entire habitat that will eventually develop into, perhaps, a global business. Getting to the locus inspires insight about how to best satisfy customers' needs and stimulates intuition that motivates evaluation and improvement of satisfactory outcomes.

At DHL Worldwide, for example, we owned or leased considerable space in airport locations around the world. Hundreds of jets and countless ground vehicles bore our name. Our logo could be found on major buildings and suitably impressive offices on all inhabited continents. But none of these "marked locations" were the true locus of our business habitat. We began by understanding our customer. That was our spark of life as a company.

Q: Let me interrupt for moment. Many corporations have the philosophy, "Build it and they will come"—that is, construct an attractive business in the form of a high-profile building with associated media hype and customers will line up at the door.

That's a risk I have never been willing to take in my own life as a business and civic leader. Harkening back to my days at the fisheries of Northern California, we would not think of building an aquatic habitat, choosing a water temperature, adjusting the water chemistry, and then dumping the fish into that habitat to see if they would survive.

The true process—and the sane one, I believe—is just the reverse: we studied the needs of particular fish, and everything else that eventually became their habitat proceeded from what we learned about those needs.

It takes a certain degree of humility to begin any venture with a thorough investigation of what your customer wants and needs. In the flush of excitement over a new business idea, it's always tempting from an ego perspective to flaunt one's new business concept as quickly and glamorously as possible. As you say, buildings pop up and expensive full-page ads appear as if those actions marked the birth of the company.

In fact, if the customers' needs aren't understood in depth, no amount of concrete poured at prestigious addresses will create a sustainable habitat.

Q: Habitats, you're suggesting, have a nature and shape of their own, depending on the profile of the customer.

Yes, but I'll quibble with your phrase, "profile of the customer." That sounds so sterile and quasi-scientific—something you could purchase from the research arm of a marketing company. It's like Internet dating—although I hasten to add that I'm guessing here: the profile you may see online may be quite different than your authentic experience with that person on a first date.

But to your point: the shape or nature of a habitat does rise directly from contact between the habitat designer and the customer. To that extent, the customer could be considered a co-designer of the habitat, even though their names may never appear on the office door.

I compare the true locus of a habitat to the fractal sets discovered by Mandelbrot. His unique insight was, simply put, that "zooming in" on a complex natural structure revealed a repeated and elementary fractal design that constituted the core building block of the larger structure. Conversely, "zooming out" revealed the eventual "shape" of that larger structure, whether in the form of a tree, mountain, river, or human face that grew out of conglomerated variations of those fractal sets.

Q: What are some examples of businesses that have used a "locus" moment of customer inquiry to dictate the eventual shape of their habitats?

Well, DHL springs to mind, but more about that later. Take Mary Kay Cosmetics, for example—a worldwide enterprise with 2010 revenue of USD $2.2 billion that began with a spark, a "locus" moment, between the target customer and the entrepreneur. In the early 1960s, Mary Kay Ash took the time to talk to real women in various locales about their skincare needs and preferences.

At that time, most skin and beauty products were sold through drugstores and supermarkets. The customer received little help, if any, in choosing products and in any case was usually dealing with a complete stranger (a teenage drugstore clerk, for example) in transactions involving intimate and sensitive issues surrounding skin blemishes and other beauty-related problems.

The "locus" moment for Mary Kay Ash came in her realization that the customer didn't just want to buy a skin cream. She (and now he as well in the Mary Kay line of products) wanted to discuss very personal needs and desires (such as the clearing of acne and other embarrassing skin problems) with a trusted peer, not a stranger.

Moreover, Mary Kay learned from her target customers that they didn't want to have that intimate conversation in the aisle of their drugstore or supermarket. Ideally, they preferred to talk about and resolve their skin issues in the privacy and trust environment of their own homes.

With that "locus" moment of insight, Mary Kay Ash realized that she didn't have to rent bricks-and-mortar space in expensive malls or struggle for shelf space for her products at drugstores and supermarkets. All she had to do was to let her initial "fractal"—the desire of the customer for at-home, confidential discussion of skin issues and product purchases—expand exponentially into the shape of her eventual business habitat (at this point, a business icon and empire).

She chose women representatives not unlike herself—good listeners who themselves had faced and solved skin problems—to visit with customers in the privacy of their homes and present an array of products to resolve the beauty care issues that came up in conversation. For many customers, their Mary Kay representative quickly became more "friend" than "vendor."

My point in this example should be obvious: ego temptations for a big building did not drive Mary Kay's inspiration for her stunningly successful enterprise. Instead, the simple "locus" moment of understanding her customers' needs gave shape to all that followed.

Q: You said "examples." Does another come to mind?

Dozens, but let me recount the story of Lockheed Martin's "locus" moment before going into more detail about DHL's own evolution from a spark of customer insight.

In the 1980s, Lockheed Martin competed with other major manufacturers of commercial and military hardware for large-scale sales to airlines and governments. In those days, aircraft were sold much the way automobiles are still sold today. The finished product was presented to top customer decision-makers in "fly-off" competitions in which the merits of Lockheed products could be compared head-on-head with those of Boeing, General Dynamics, and other aerospace giants.

Lockheed won its share of competitions, but to its dismay also lost some competitions (expensively so) that it thought it had "in the bag." Instead of licking its wounds and going back to the design drawing boards, Lockheed executives packed their bags and went on a "listening tour" of commercial airline sites and military bases. What they learned surprised them and revolutionized Lockheed's approach to its business.

Their "locus" moment came when potential customers told Lockheed executives, "Look, we like your product. It's probably the best out there. But we didn't buy it because you don't help us fly it or fix it. You're asking us to spend hundreds of millions of dollars on hardware that we don't begin to understand. There's no training or user's manual!"

Lockheed got it. Previously, they thought they were in the business of making and selling jets. After this listening tour, they realized they were in the business of enabling their customers to fly and fix Lockheed products. An entire new division of the company focused on training materials and programs sprung up within Lockheed.

In less than a year, motivated by Lockheed's response to customer input, most airlines and governments established purchasing regulations specifying that no significant hardware (including jets) could be purchased without an accompanying training package for pilots, mechanics, and others responsible for the functioning of that equipment. The "shape" of

Lockheed as a corporation changed dramatically as a result of a "locus" moment with its customers.

Q: Tell us about your own "locus" moment with DHL's explosive growth in Asia.

Let me answer that, for simplicity, by saying "I" in this answer. Of course, the actual fact was that "we"—a number of us tasked with expanding DHL into Asia—were simultaneously involved under my leadership in what I will describe.

From my earlier experience in the toy manufacturing and distribution business in Hong Kong, I knew that product excellence alone was an inadequate base upon which to build a growing business or shape a sustainable habitat. Interaction with customers, as any good salesman can tell you, is at least 50 percent of any successful sales effort.

In transitioning to the courier business—an enterprise that had no "product" as such—I knew that even more weight would fall upon understanding and responding to customers' service needs. Therefore, I took the time—a lot of time—to roll up my sleeves, loosen my tie, and walk the client neighborhoods that DHL intended to serve. I engaged potential customers in conversation not by telling them how great DHL was or what it had already achieved in Europe and the U.S. Instead, I asked them what they needed from a courier and delivery service.

There was surprising unanimity in what I heard from future customers, and that common voice from our target clients gave me confidence that a thriving courier business could be built in Hong Kong and throughout Asia.

First, customers told me, they needed reliability. Documents (DHL's primary item for delivery) had to arrive on time for the closing of real estate deals, the resolution of legal proceedings, the confirmation of financial dealings, and a wealth of other business matters. A day late, for whatever reason, wouldn't cut it with these customers.

Second, they needed to be confident in the security of what they sent and received. "Lost in the mail" was an excuse they had agonized over for years with other document delivery agents; a new courier service would have to strive for 100 percent security for shipments through hi-tech tracking methods and rigid internal security procedures.

Finally, they wanted an end to "red tape." Previous delivery channels, including the Post Office, too often delivered a story—"held up at Customs" or "delayed at the docks"—rather than delivering the package. DHL, as the new kid on the block, would have to work not only with its customers but also with all the roadblocks, regulations, and gatekeepers that stood in the way of efficient and dependable package delivery.

Interestingly, agreeing to the price point for our services was a lower priority in our customers' list of requirements. The deals involved in the documents and other packages we were delivering were sufficiently large and profitable that a few percentage points higher or lower in the courier's rate wasn't the primary determinant of choice of server. Customers wanted a company they could count on, and were willing to pay for that level of excellent service.

I came away from these customer conversations with a mixture of optimism and downright anxiety. On the up side, I was no longer naïve about what it would take to succeed as a business. My customers informed me and I understood, in our "locus" moment together, exactly what they wanted.

On the down side, my job had suddenly become more complex than I had imagined. I needed to become an amateur lobbyist and politician of sorts in streamlining the process by which both local and international packages of all kinds "made it through" the existing maze of regulations, customs inspections, and other hurdles.

The habitat for an Asian expansion of DHL began to take a new shape in my mind. From my spark of insight with real customers, I glimpsed a habitat positioned to change the external system of regulation without becoming an overt enemy to that system.

Specifically, that meant that DHL personnel at all levels had to "massage" the existing channels of regulation rather than bark angrily at them. We wanted government officials, customs agents, and others in the path of our progress to view DHL as easy to work with, eager to get the job done well, and intelligent in offering patient suggestions for improving the delivery process in all its dimensions.

In short, DHL positioned itself to make external agents "look good" rather than casting them as hopeless bureaucrats or hapless bunglers.

I must say that this positioning didn't happen by the issuing of a corporate "white paper" or a series of ads in the business news. In the same way that I had my "locus" moment with customers, each DHL representative down to the most junior courier was encouraged by the DHL habitat and culture to send the right message of friendliness, cooperation, and appropriate patience when they interfaced with external players in the entire network of delivery. After all, if customs officials became "pissed off" (pardon the expression) at what they perceived as "pushy" DHL couriers, these people could ruin our efforts to deliver on time.

Q: I need to understand one detail of the habitat-building process. Does a large habitat like the eventual DHL Worldwide culture emerge from an initial spark or "locus" moment, or are new moments and insights influencing the company habitat repeatedly and continually?

Definitely the latter. Referring once more to our fishery example, we needed to monitor the health of the fish on a regular basis and, if problems appeared, to make immediate changes in the habitat environment.

Similarly at DHL, our "locus" moments potentially could occur every time a courier interacted with a customer or, for that matter, whenever members of our entire team interacted with one another.

We casually called this "understanding the monkey on each other's back." A courier held up by a sorting or tracking problem at an airport or other DHL facility couldn't just shrug and tell the customer, "Oops there." Instead, he or she had to locate the problem (or turn to tech people who could locate it), sound off about it to people who could fix it, and check up to make sure that problem didn't recur. These were all internal "locus" moments that shaped the habitat into an environment confident in its abilities to solve problems of all kinds.

Because everyone within the habitat took on the responsibility of being a problem reporter and problem solver, we all had to agree (and remind each other often) that personalities were on the sidelines. Any problem was a business matter, not a personal jab. Members of the habitat understood that we would make little progress in problem-solving if constructive criticism was misinterpreted as a personal attack.

I must say that not all companies are so fortunate in their habitats. The last decade has seen the collapse of global giants such as Enron. If you peeked inside the habitats of these business super-novae, almost inevitably you would observe a spoken or unspoken "code of silence" when it came to calling out problems that might make your supervisor or others above you in the food chain "look bad." Saving face came at the expense of not serving the customer or other stakeholders. With considerable irony, in too many cases saving face meant losing the company itself.

To sum up for a moment, a habitat can be viewed as an elastic bag. It expands, contracts, and changes shape according to the events that take place within it (that is, events that involve its internal team) as well as developments external to the habitat, such as market changes, governmental regulation, and regional crises such as the recent environmental tragedy in Japan.

Q: We have a clear picture of the birth of a business habitat, based on customer needs. Let's move on to discuss its design and architecture.

As I mentioned at the outset of today's conversation, many skilled hands and minds have been at work over the last several decades in showing how successful business structures can be built and monitored. We could literally fill this room with books on the various aspects of building and running a business. I referred earlier to a handful of the leading scions in this area.

But I also promised to shed whatever insight I can into the less discussed but no less important aspects of habitat development and maintenance—the topics on which not much has been written to date.

First, every habitat large or small has a circulatory system of sorts made up of communication veins and arteries. I'll drop the analogy there for the sake of aesthetics, but you can picture what I am talking about: a vast and complicated series of interconnections between people through which communications of all kinds flow back and forth.

The key question—and an issue that is just starting to be discussed among management theorists and practitioners—is the issue of "communication architecture." In previous decades, the plumbing of company headquarters received infinitely more time, money, and attention than did the much more crucial matter of communication channels.

By channels, I am talking about much more than the nature of a company's IT equipment, although that's part of the picture. Instead, I'm raising the basic question of "who talks to whom, and about what?". Traditionally, this question has been ignored almost entirely in the growth of a business habitat. Communication has been allowed to grow (or not) like weeds in the garden—a haphazard tangle of so-called connections between people that, like the old telephone circuits, sometimes worked and sometimes didn't.

Pick any organization that you consider dysfunctional to some degree—perhaps an organization in which you have worked and know well. As you put the issue of person-to-person communication under the microscope, you discover many malignancies. In an unplanned, no-architect communication culture, at least five malfunctions can usually be observed:

- some people are forbidden by company culture from talking to others in the company. Here I refer to the quasi-military code of never "talking out of school" or "over the head" of one's immediate supervisor. In these business habitats, the supervisor becomes the de facto "lid" on information that passes upward to company decision-makers. In most cases, information that may tend to make a supervisor's work unit look bad is suppressed entirely, and perhaps with punishment for the "whistleblower" who brought the information forward.

Conversely, information which makes the supervisor's unit look good is often magnified and distorted in its importance when it makes its way to the top of the organization. In both cases, it's no wonder that decisions often go awry, based as they are on skewed data from biased and repressive gatekeepers at lower levels in the organization.

- communication pipelines are established but nothing useful flows through them. Infamous in this regard are "suggestion boxes" (usually electronic rather than physical these days) set up with great pomp and circumstance by company leaders, but summarily ignored by everyone thereafter. In effect, the establishment of a suggestion system becomes just a token that company leaders feel should "be there," much like a knick-knack shelf in a living room—furniture, ignored and useless, except for an occasional mandatory dusting.

In earlier corporate days when suggestion boxes were physical wooden boxes placed in company hallways, employees could easily see that any suggestion stuffed into a box was still there after a week, a month, or more. That nonverbal message was both telling and chilling: the company wanted the illusion of employee input but not the reality.

Electronic suggestion systems don't allow employees to see that their contents are not "emptied," much less read—and this lack of transparency compounds the question of whether the company really cares about employee ideas. The same can be said of the endless employee surveys pumped out by HR units within major organizations—surveys that are usually ignored by employees unless they are compelled to fill them out by their bosses with the result of highly suspect sincerity in such forced data. What ever came about as a consequence of the survey we took? That's the question employees can't help but ask, especially when the survey touched on issues important to employee satisfaction.

- "bandwidth" of communication channels is ill-designed and managed. Communication, in its conversion from data (typically black and white marks on a page) to meaning (ideas within the mind), takes *time*, not just good intentions.

A CEO, for example, may grandly offer an "open door policy" to any employee any time. But lacking some design for his or her executive time, this offer is a gross underestimation of bandwidth. In a company of several thousand employees, does the CEO really expect to give even a modest amount of time to conversation with *anyone* in the company? What if even ten percent of the thousands of employees in the company actually took the CEO up on his or her offer?

The grand gesture of an open door would quickly be revealed as a "take-a-ticket-for-two-months-from-now" policy, and result in one more disillusioning interaction between levels of company hierarchy.

- the unofficial "grapevine" gains more credibility and attention than official company communication channels. Once employees conclude that so-called communication outreach efforts by upper management are exclusively for "show" purposes, these workers invent and jealously guard their own communication network—the "grapevine."

Members of the grapevine, which strictly excludes management, gain status by information, rumors, and downright gossip they can contribute. It is as if all members to the grapevine were avid viewers of the same Facebook page to which only they had access.

Once the grapevine gains transcendency in credibility over company information sources, managers are hard pressed to communicate the "truth" of company events, plans, and prospects to their employees, no matter how urgent the matter. If employees are convinced by the grapevine that layoffs are coming, motivation may plummet—or, on the other hand, employees may become fiercely and destructively competitive with one another in an effort to avoid the fall of the layoff axe on their own necks.

• unplanned communication also results in poorly timed communication, with devastating results for employee morale. As within family, important news (let's say, the engagement of a daughter to be married) has to go out to all members of the family at about the same time, lest anyone have their "feelings hurt."

Translated into corporate reality, important company news that reaches the Marketing Department two weeks before the Finance Department hears about it is a sure recipe for disgruntlement, strained relations between the two departments, and antagonism toward the corporate leader who distributed the information in such an unplanned way. Workers cannot help but conclude that "knowledge is power"—and those last to receive the knowledge are those last in line for power in the organization.

For all these reasons, communication architecture for the company habitat has to be an early and continuing priority in its growth and development.

First, and above all, communication channels should be real and practical. If upper level management solicits regular input from the rank-and-file through surveys, suggestion boxes, or focus groups, this offer is a *commitment* that must be backed up by a) devoting necessary time and resources to accomplish it ("bandwidth"); b) actually doing it; and c) having something come of it in terms of feedback from leadership and possible company action.

Second, communication should be designed in such a way that it can be monitored. I'm not talking here about secretly reading the emails and text messages that pass between employees. Instead, I'm referring to regular checks on which communication channels are flowing and which are choked or blocked entirely. We certainly would respond quickly to such problems with the company plumbing system!

Company leadership needs to know if all units in the company have access to the information they need to do their jobs. Many cross-industry surveys reveal that employees suspect that their managers withhold information necessary to successful job performance.

Leaders have to feel the pulse of email loads and response times: are employees deluged by so many emails that they end up skipping even the most important? Is the "cc:" and "bcc:" function of email abused in the company so the majority of email messages received by an employee have no relevance to his or her job? Has a culture of "I'll-get-to-it-tomorrow" set in, whereby emails sit for days on end waiting for a response, usually with the excuse "I have too much email to wade through each day and it just piles up."

Finally, communication architecture must consider its full range of options and maximize the impact of each. Are meeting occurring simply because "it's Monday and we always have the Monday morning meeting." Are meetings successful as sessions for discussion, information transfer, and decision-making—or are they boring rituals where the same individuals drone on and on, interrupted occasionally by the loud yawns of other members? Peter Drucker's quip is apropos: "We can meet or we can work. We can't do both at the same time."

In addition to efficient meeting management and monitoring, does the company have attractive, up-to-date channels of communication to supplant (and often counteract) the rumors flying on the employee grapevine? Such channels can include a company newsletter, magazine, e-letter from the company president, regular email briefings, and an FAQ site (always kept current) on the internal company website.

The mechanics of communication architecture for growing and managing a habitat are common sense. You can literally sketch out how communication should ideally flow within the company, avoiding the naïve assumption that "everyone will be able to talk with everyone". Pay particular attention to the following issues:

- what channels are best suited for particular communications in terms of need-to-know, message security, and prioritization, so that the company leader is not inundated with copies of every message that passes within the company—and then expected to respond in some way to each!

- what purpose a particular form of communication is intended to serve–for example, a purely informational fact sheet versus a spirit-rousing, largely symbolic keynote speech by the CEO at the annual company meeting.

- who is responsible for monitoring and maintaining the health of the communication system, with regular feedback from all users ("Are you able to communicate as you need to?" "What communication obstacles are you encountering?" "What kinds of communication would help you do your job better?").

Q: What about companies that have widely dispersed workers?

Communication became a special challenge in a company like DHL, where our most valuable and accurate sources of customer information and feedback were "in the field" as couriers most of the day and largely out of contact with company decision-makers. Of course, they had data contact with their dispatcher, but this channel was not typically used for registering suggestions, customer issues, observation of new market possibilities, and so forth.

However, time given to regular debriefing of field couriers by their field manager was not considered wasted "downtime" at DHL. These end-of-the-day, during-the-day, or end-of-the-week conversations, whether in person or by phone or other means, set in motion an extremely useful "filter up" flow of communication that allowed the company to remain nimble in responding both to customer problems and to market changes. Simultaneously, couriers felt more pride in their positions as integral problem-solvers within the company.

Q: How did company executives like yourself feel about passing power, so to speak, to the base of the hierarchy?

For all its appearance of relative prestige, white collar work behind an expensive desk was not hallowed at DHL as the "spark" place where Jehovah's finger touched Adam's. Those of us who led the company knew how much we depended not only on the stamina and integrity of our field couriers and their managers, but also on their intelligence in listening for valuable customer information and their diligence—and sometime courage, in the case of bad news—-in passing this information up to where it could be addressed in a system-wide way.

Whenever possible, we tried to avoid the "bandaid" phenomena of patching up little problems but never connecting the dots to see what larger issues these symptoms were depicting. Our typical response, let's say, to a glitch observed by a few couriers was to a) check out that observation with a random sampling of our people in various regions; b) determine with their insights the cause of and suggestions for solving the problem; and c) deploy the necessary talent and resources to resolve the problem at its root rather than to mask it. Before the top levels of the company started addressing the issue, they already possessed others' "brainstormed" lists of possible causes and solutions.

My job would have been easy, of course, if all problems that crossed my desk had an obvious and affordable solution. That is seldom the case for any corporate executive. But in cases where problems were going to take time to solve or for which we had no immediate solution, we made it a practice at DHL to let stakeholders to the problem know that we were working hard on it and would be in touch with them—and then we followed through on those commitments.

Stakeholders to a problem included not only the courier(s) who reported it but also the customers who were suffering in some way from the problem. On many occasions, these customers took time to let me know that they appreciated the fact that DHL was working on the problem and that the company had the courtesy to keep them updated.

That's all part of "communication architecture" that can be consciously and purposefully built in to the habitat. If left to good intentions, such communications will be shoved to the margins of the day and happen only as an occasional after-thought rather than as an important component in corporate philosophy and strategy.

Q: To tell you the truth, the phrase "communication architecture" seems relatively new to me.

The fact that many have never heard the phrase tells you that it is ignored by most companies, and at their peril. A well-designed plan for how communication should flow within a company inevitably involves policies and procedures. Some of these are word-of-mouth and simply part of the culture.

For example, at DHL we mutually agreed by culture rather than contract not to "over-communicate." Our orientation to the culture of the company included the wisdom not to write unnecessary emails, not to copy people who had no need to know about the business at hand, not to call physical meetings that could be avoided by a couple well-placed phone calls, and above all to maintain professional courtesy in our internal and external communications, no matter how stressful or maddening the situation at hand.

Written policies that are wise for companies to commit to an employee handbook include guidelines on the private use of company communication channels and equipment ("don't phone your mother in Greece on a company phone"), definition of inappropriate materials to access on or distribute by company computers or cell phones, especially sexually-oriented items or humor that disparages race, gender, religion, sexual preference, and so forth.

Q: You've probably observed that people in leadership positions within the company are often the worst communicators.

That observation has not escaped me. A person's ability to communicate in a leadership role is especially crucial because it sets the standard for others who are "learning the ropes" and will someday be company leaders themselves.

For example, if I run a meeting but do 80 percent of the talking myself, I not only subvert the purpose of the meeting but I mis-teach everyone there that meetings should be dominated by the chairperson.

The answer to this problem begins with good hiring. A resume alone does not tell you what kind of communicator a candidate will be. I recommend that you have any candidate for a managerial position write a paragraph on the spot as part of the hiring process. If they can't put 6 to 8 sentences together in a cogent, intelligent way, there's little chance they are ever going to be able to generate an important company report or proposal.

An alternate hiring task is to give them a short article on a business topic and ask them to summarize it in writing within a paragraph or two. This task tests not only their ability to write, but also their ability to analyze, prioritize, and condense an extended argument into a shorter form. You will know immediately from this exercise if they can "get to the point."

Q: How do you evaluate the presentation skills of candidates?

In terms of oral presenting, the one-on-one or one-on-group nature of the hiring interview will give you some idea of the person's skill in presenting themselves and their points of view. But at Toastmaster's and other professional self-improvement organizations, the "table topic" technique proves valuable for observing how well an individual thinks on his or her feet.

It's worth the fifteen minutes it takes to give the candidate some reasonably interesting and general topic ("Describe two management styles and explain which you prefer"), provide a few minutes for preparation, and then see what the candidate can do. If he or she rambles, has difficulty connecting ideas, and struggles with obvious nervousness, you have significant clues about how they will perform on the job.

None of us is a perfect communicator, of course. Any company that invests in communication training for its managers is spending dollars wisely. Media training for company leadership is increasingly important, since company or industry events can put any of us in front of TV cameras on a moment's notice.

Presentation skills for the camera differ substantially from public speaking skills. Leaders need to have practice in on-camera presenting and expert feedback on how they are coming across, both for their own careers and for the image of the company.

Q: We have a clear picture of communication architecture as one area of Design that can set one business venture into "blue oceans" while others are mired in red waters. Let's move on to the second topic that's often ignored in the design stage—what you earlier called the architecture of human motivation.

Gladly. I find it helpful, when I approach a somewhat diffuse and uncharted area such as the architecture of human motivation to reduce my scope of inquiry at first to this moment, this place, and the people in it.

Here's what I mean. You are interviewing me at this moment. Let's analyze the motivation that has brought us to these chairs, in this place, at this moment, and for this activity. I can speak candidly about my primary motivators and guess a bit about yours.

I'm motivated to be here today by the self-fulfillment and satisfying sense of giving that I feel in sharing my thoughts about the DNA of service sector businesses. I know that a book will emerge from this extended conversation, and I picture that book doing some good in the world for students and practitioners of service businesses. This motivation is sufficiently strong that I can say sincerely that I would be doing this interview activity even if there were no hope for financial profit in the form of book royalties.

Q: And what do you see as my motives in being here as your interviewer?

You, too, have largely altruistic motives in undertaking this work. After all, you could be doing a sure-fire bestseller in the form of a diet book or cookbook. Aren't those the "cash cows" of the publishing industry? But instead, you're willing to explore "blue oceans" with me in developing a conversational guide to the global service sector.

What's more, we seem to have enjoyed our conversations thus far, spanning a number of days. In other words, the line between work and play has been pleasantly blurred for you and for me. I can't say that I would be enjoying a game of tennis more than I am enjoying this conversation about topics that arouse my business imagination and passion.

From a publisher's point of view, I suspect it is equally fun for you to be on the cutting edge instead of the butcher's block of business topics.

Q: Indeed it is. You've put your finger on the key motivators that brought me to this creative endeavor. Speak more generally, please, about what you've called the architecture of human motivation.

In the same way that we took a moment to analyze why we're here now and what keeps us here through the completion of this book project, so a person involved in the Design stage of a service sector business, or any business, for that matter, has to ask "what keeps them working well and coming back tomorrow."

In tough economic times, the first answer that leaps to mind is "money," pure and simple. When several people are available for every job that gets filled, it's tempting to build our architecture of human motivation on the assumption that people work, and keep working, just to pay their bills and maybe get ahead a little.

In fact, that assumption proves to be a shaky foundation for a sustainable architecture of human motivation. In work begun by Lindahl and carried out frequently in recent decades by management gurus Paul Hersey and

Kenneth Blanchard, supervisors and regular workers were asked to rate on a scale of 1 to 10 (1 being their highest preference) what they identified as their motivators for sticking with a particular job.[10]

The results perpetually surprise those who believe that money alone is the great motivator for employees. In Hersey and Blanchard's most recent study of 10,000 employees across industry sectors, it turns out that "wages" on average are ranked 5 by workers. Much more important to them, in terms of work motivation, are "being in on things" (ranked 2), receiving "appreciation" for what they do (ranked 1), and having their "personal problems understood" by the boss (ranked 3).

These studies give us an entirely different picture of how we might design a workable architecture for human motivation. We quickly disabuse ourselves of the notion that a fair wage with modest raises each year will attract good employees and keep our best workers from moving on. Instead, we need to contemplate an architecture not unlike the one we said that we ourselves were enjoying during these conversations—an architecture that appeals not primarily to financial needs but also to deeply human needs. It turns out that rewarding team members with psychic income is a low-cost and effective way to increase loyalty, commitment, productivity, and profit.

In this regard, just as a supporting footnote of sorts, be aware that virtually all the data on why people quit their jobs has to do with interpersonal factors—"I couldn't get along with my boss," "I didn't feel like I was part of the team"—rather than money matters. Workers are much more influenced by their social relationships at work than are supervisors. For example, supervisors rank "appreciation" as "8" out of 10 (10 being lowest) and "being in on things" as "10" on their list of what they want from their jobs. Of course, managers of services may well value these factors differently, and research is now underway to determine if this is true.

Q: This may be a naïve question, but why bother to build an architecture of human motivation at all? Don't these things sort themselves out according to each individual's personality?

We design an architecture for worker motivation for the same reason we take the time to design a communication architecture. Ignoring the "engine" (that is, the motivation) that drives worker effort within the company or leaving it to chance is as foolish as turning a construction crew loose to build a high-rise tower without any blueprints. When it comes to design thinking, we definitely "reap what we sow"—and in planning an architecture for human motivation, we give ourselves the best opportunity to assemble and retain a skilled, gung-ho workforce.

Q: So what motivates workers in the service industry to get up each morning and put in an honest day's work?

Abraham Maslow asked that essential question in his hierarchy of human needs. The core logic of his pyramid, sketched here, is that certain basic needs must be fulfilled before a person turns his or her attention to satisfying what Maslow calls "higher order" needs. What Maslow proposes is as true of the service sector as any aspect of business.[11]

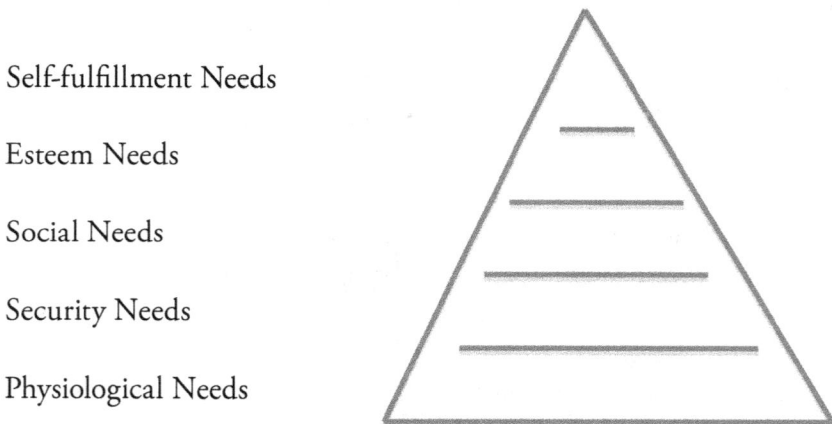

Self-fulfillment Needs

Esteem Needs

Social Needs

Security Needs

Physiological Needs

Figure 1. Hierarchy of Human Needs

The mistake that many businesses make in thinking about work motivation is that they "flatten" Maslow's pyramid. They look upon worker motivation as if it consisted of nothing beyond Physiological needs, which are primarily satisfied by the weekly or monthly paycheck. This could be viewed as the "pancake" syndrome, in that it minimizes the importance of all higher-order human needs and maximizes the supposed importance of pay alone.

A more sophisticated, useful, and effective architecture for human motivation considers all the higher levels of Maslow's hierarchy. We should be asking, "How can these human needs be systematically addressed in our design for human motivation in the company?"

Q: That suggests a pretty complicated architecture, doesn't it? Aren't you trying to design separate motivational schemes for a wide variety of groups in the company?

Certainly the design I'm proposing is more complicated than the "pancake" approach of considering only the motivational value of the paycheck! But let me choose two areas of the architecture we are discussing to give you a concrete idea of how they can become part of the "pull" that keeps workers happy and loyal, with a focus on the service sector.

First, consider motivation by expectation. To some extent, we all "live for tomorrow"—that is, we do our jobs today in expectation that our efforts will lead to desired benefits of some kind in the future. We do this not only for ourselves but also for the "significant others" in our lives.

This future-oriented motivation can be built into our design by recognizing that new, entry-level employees may need to "see results" more obviously and more frequently than seasoned veterans. The motivational needs of new employees can be viewed in this way:

goal-directed activities ———> GOAL-FULFILLMENT ACTIVITIES

In other words, what looms large (in capital letters) on the radar of new employees are tangible signs of success rather than the day-to-day work of goal-directed activities. For this reason, virtually all fast-food companies (employing countless millions of young people around the planet) give a series of small raises rather quickly within the employee's first year, along with ego-boosting title promotions. These companies recognize that new employees are likely to quit if their efforts aren't acknowledged early and regularly. The amount of the raise—let's say, USD $6.50 raised to $6.75—may seem trivial. But new workers see this Goal-Fulfillment marker as a sign that they are appreciated, that they are a step ahead of the "newbies" who entered the company after they did, and that they are making progress on the job. In short, they feel good about themselves and have something to brag about to their parents and others.

Old hands in the company, however, are motivated by a different scenario:

GOAL-DIRECTED ACTIVITIES ————> goal-fulfillment activities

They don't need small monthly raises or frequent, progressive changes in job titles to keep their nose to the grindstone. Consequently, they are able to go for longer periods with their focus on (and satisfaction from) goal-directed activities, capitalized here to indicate the importance they place on this aspect of their work. In effect, they tell themselves that doing a good job day-in and day-out will eventually bring significant goal-fulfillment in the form of an annual bonus, a meaningful promotion, or "winning the company trip."

If you buy into this vision of new-worker motivation versus experienced-worker motivation, you should plan for it within the architecture of your motivational design. You give small but quick and regular ego-boosters to new employees (whether in the form of money raises, commendations, Employee of the Week pins, and so forth). At the same time, you design your motivational system for experienced employees very differently, knowing that they are "in it" for the long-haul and don't want or need the same frequency of ego-boosters as do junior employees.

Q: It sounds as if new employees are less willing or able to take on long-term challenges compared to seasoned employees. After all, working on a significant job challenge can require long periods of few rewards, or what you call goal-directed activities.

As a general rule, I believe that's true—although occasionally a new employee surprises you with his or her ability to delay immediate satisfiers while working on long-term projects. The motivational aspects of work challenges were studied in depth by McClelland and Atkinson. Their research yielded their famous "50 Percent Curve":[12]

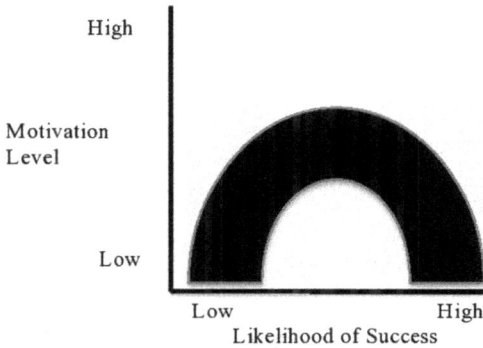

Figure 2. Human motivation rises with the likelihood of success, but falls off as success becomes a sure thing.

This chart depicts their finding that workers across industries are increasingly motivated as their probability of success rises. But at a certain point (around 50 percent in their analysis), motivation begins to fall off if the probability of success becomes increasingly assured.

In companies we recognize this motivational decline as the "retirement" syndrome. Within a year or two of retirement, employees may feel they have their jobs "wired" and that now it's just a matter of marking time and treading water until retirement day. In other words, their probability of success is assured—there's no challenge left because there's no realistic chance of failure. They tell their friends they are coasting "on the downward slope" toward retirement—echoing exactly the findings of McClelland and Atkinson.

The "50 Percent Curve" alerts design thinkers that they should build challenges and a certain degree of uncertainty (including permissible failure) into their motivational architecture. An interesting way of conceiving this motivational phenomenon can be seen in the common yard game of quoits (where rings are tossed over a peg). As demonstrated by carefully controlled experiments, people who are given a handful of rings and told to "throw them over the peg" tend to create their own scenario of play and challenge. Obviously they could stand right over the peg and successfully drop all rings onto it.

But interestingly, they don't. They move back from the peg to a distance that they individually define as their "challenge zone"—that is, the range that makes the activity stimulating. If they get one out of three rings onto the peg from their challenge zone, they feel they have "won" in the sense that they have met the challenge they defined for themselves.

Notice that people do not tend to move so far back from the peg that getting even one ring onto it becomes nearly impossible. In terms of the "50 Percent Curve," that arrangement would be comparable to positioning oneself at the "Low" end of probability of success, yielding low motivation to even try.

Q: I don't have any quoits or pegs handy, but apply your description of this game to motivation architecture in the service sector.

In designing an architecture for successful human motivation, managers have to build interesting but not impossible challenges into people's jobs. Making a job too easy ("shooting fish in a barrel") will yield low motivation because success is assured and there's no sense of achievement in facing and conquering a challenge. On the other hand, making a challenge too difficult will exhaust the patience and energies of even the best employee, who inevitably gives up trying because the chances of success are so low.

Q: You mentioned the "f" word—"failure." That's not a popular word in business.
Agreed. I guess the current euphemisms are "limited success" or "lack of complete achievement." Call it what you will, failure is not automatically the enemy of motivation (as revealed in the "50 Percent Curve") but instead

is an integral component of any worthwhile work challenge. Of course, the certainty of failure is demotivating in the extreme. But the *possibility* of failure can be arousing and stimulating—the "spice" that makes an activity challenging. The chance of failure, by analogy, is the hurdle that makes the race exciting.

We are all by nature problem-solvers to one degree or another. By definition, a problem is an unresolved situation or dilemma—that is, a circumstance that through our efforts can turn out positively ("success") or negatively ("failure"), or some mixture of the two. When companies penalize failure too severely, they discourage employees from taking on any challenges that involve the *possibility* of failure as, of course, virtually all real challenges do.

Therefore, a sound design for motivational architecture has to make clear that failure in bona fide attempts to meet work challenges does not spell the end of the world. As we tell our young children, "Pick yourself up, dust yourself off, and try again." Freed from the stigma of failure as an albatross around their necks and a complete loss of status among their peers, employees will be much more likely to take on tough tasks and give it their best.

To sum up this mini-sermon on motivation by expectation, let me try to cite the work of Victor Vroom, who in many ways is the "father" of expectancy theory.[13] Vroom has a clever way of determining if a person will be motivated on the job. It goes like this:

> If you believe that your effort positively affects your work performance
> and
> If you believe that your work performance leads to predictable outcomes
> and
> If you value those outcomes,
> then
> Your motivation at work will be maximized.

Q: Catchy, but give us an example.

Sure. Let's say that a DHL courier recognizes that his hard work (effort) is getting him high marks in terms of job performance. Further, this courier trusts that the company will provide certain rewards for those high marks. Moreover, he values those rewards (whether in the form of raises, job promotion, widespread recognition in the company, and so forth). Under these conditions, we can expect this courier to maintain high levels of motivation.

But take away any of Vroom's three factors and motivation plummets. Let's say, for example, that the courier doesn't believe that DHL will reward his good performance. Motivation slips. Or let's say that, by good fortune, he finds himself independently wealthy through an inheritance and no longer values the financial rewards that DHL will give him for top performance. Again, motivation slips.

Q: So that's motivation by expectation. You mentioned a second, often-untried form of employee motivation.

Yes. In the literature of motivation theory, this second approach is called "equity" motivation. It operates according to a common-sense formula—a concept we've all experienced in our work lives:[14]

$$\frac{\text{Your effort}}{\text{Your reward}} \quad \text{should equal} \quad \frac{\text{My effort}}{\text{My reward}}$$

Instead of a courier, let's take the situation of two scanners responsible for electronically logging in and out the thousands of DHL packages that pass through a large airport facility. One scanner works the heavy day shift, with many more jet arrivals to cope with and frequently extended hours. The other scanner works the lighter night shift, where work flow is relatively predictable with periods of down-time between plane arrivals.

It happens that the night scanner (through the grapevine) discovers that he is making 10 percent less than the day-time scanner, even though they both joined the company at the same time. How does he feel about this situation? It doesn't eat at his liver because he says to himself, in effect, "Hey, I've got the easy shift and he's got the hard shift. I understand why he gets a little more money." In other words, "my effort" divided by "my reward" is in approximate balance (that is, equity) to "his effort" divided by "his reward."

But reverse that situation: the hard-working day-time scanner discovers that the night scanner is earning 10 percent more than he does. Now "the force" is definitely disturbed, in *Star Wars* language. The day-time scanner tells all who will listen, "It just isn't fair! I'm working my butt off during the hard shift while he's sitting on his during the easy shift. Why should he be earning more than I do?"

Q: This must happen all the time in business when people inevitably find out what others earn in the company. How does their discovery affect motivation?

People respond in interesting ways. To adjust the equity scales, the lower-paid but harder working scanner in our example might march to the manager's office and request a pay raise, with the implied threat that he will be looking for another job if the raise is not forthcoming. In this scanner's mind, the raise would adjust the equity balance in Adams' scale above. His side of the equation would be amplified by an increase in his reward.

The same scanner might attempt to adjust the equity balance in another, more negative way. He could say to himself (and others), "If I'm earning less, by God I'm going to give less." Without consciously thinking about Adams or any formula, he instinctively reasons that he will give less effort to the job and thus "pay back" the company for the inequity he perceives.

These assertive, even aggressive behaviors are typical of extrovert personalities at work. More introverted types might turn to an ego defense mechanism— tuning out information that one finds distressful. An introverted worker might say to himself, "All kinds of rumors about pay are spread around by the grapevine everyday. You never know whom to believe. Besides, the guy who says he is earning more than I do is a loud-mouth and probably is just making up a story to aggravate me."

By resorting to ego defense mechanisms, we push away the irritants in our lives and just go on with our work. Motivation, however, is certainly not *increased* in an employee living with nagging doubts about the fairness of his compensation or status.

Q: *You described the motivational effects on the person who drew the short straw. How is motivation affected for those who are on the "up" side of the equity equation?*

Research is mixed on this issue. You can locate highly paid individuals—the "superstars" or "rainmakers" of the organization—who are motivated to give maximum effort to the company as a public way of showing they "deserve" their large salaries and bonuses, and perhaps as a personal, internal commitment to be true to their own work ethic.

But "making it" (as the "50 Percent Curve" suggests) can also breed laziness and lack of motivation. In some civil service jobs, for example, "tenure" of sorts is awarded after a certain number of years. Employees holding such tenure are at the "top of the heap" and may no longer feel the "excitement of the chase" or the eagerness they once felt to achieve their next promotion.

In a word, they are no longer "hungry"—and their work performance shows it.

KEY POINTS

1. Contemporary business studies tend to focus on manufacturing cases and concepts, even though most urban trading centers are primarily made up of service industries and professions.

2. The DNA of service sector businesses and service occupations and the ways that DNA expresses itself in thinking and behavior is distinctly different from that of manufacturing companies and jobs. Understanding the service sector requires a "curriculum" not presently available in most business schools and corporate training centers.

3. Service is the crucible of entrepreneurship—the industry sector in which experimentation, adaptation, human relations, and performance feedback are tested in the fires of the customer's high expectations.

4. Because the vital interests of many stakeholders are involved, service requires that its providers have a well-honed "personal operating system" in terms of their professional ethics and personal character.

5. The main spiritual traditions of both East and West can prove valuable to understanding human needs as well as service options available to address and satisfy the needs of one's customers.

6. In Eastern spiritual traditions, Buddhism tends to offer guidance for individual growth and insight; Confucianism for harmonious, productive relationships with others; and Taoism for "big picture" perspectives about the nature of human enterprise and the influence of universal processes on human behavior.

7. A "liberal imagination" is a pre-requisite for achieving original designs for service businesses and careers. This imagination is developed by a wide variety of aesthetic, experiential, philosophical, and practical activities that free the mind to play with its full range of design options.

8. A service enterprise must be designed so that it finds its own space in "blue oceans" rather than being restricted to traditional, "red oceans" thinking.

9. Conscious design efforts provide an opportunity for model-building and idea testing before enormous amounts of company resources are poured into buildings, salaries, marketing, and other expenses.

10. The design of a company's communication architecture as well as the design of its human motivation architecture are too often ignored in the rush toward hiring, building, publicizing, and rolling out company services.

11. The "locus" or spark of life for a company's initial development of its habitat lies in getting to know its target customers and their business needs.

12. Businesses as varied as Mary Kay Cosmetics and Lockheed Martin have demonstrated the power of knowing one's customer as an absolute pre-requisite for design of the company habitat and services.

13. "Locus" moments for company development happen often throughout all levels of the company, producing an evolutionary pattern of organizational development.

14. Communication architecture is a design feature that specifies channels of communication, "bandwidth" for communication recipients, methods for monitoring the efficiency of communication flow, and cultural standards for preventing communication overload.

15. A widely dispersed workforce poses special challenges for any company committed to soliciting "bottom up" communication from field representatives.

16. The design of human motivation for service sector companies includes lessons from Maslow's Hierarchy of Needs, expectancy theory, and equity theory.

Chapter Four

Build: An Entrepreneur's Guide to Creating What Matters Most

Q: In our last session, you outlined the "think work" that needs to go into any successful service organization before staff is hired and facilities are acquired. You also made the important point that such design work is on-going throughout an organization's evolution. Let's move ahead to the next component in a service company's DNA—the "build" stage. Describe what you mean by building a service organization.

We could stack up dozens of relevant books on that topic. So permit me to answer your question at first by exclusion: I'm not focusing here on the intricate process of site selection, facility architecture, contractor oversight, legal compliance, or any of the other elements that go into literally building a service organization.

Instead, I want to pinpoint what's involved in building your people—certainly the heart of any service organization. Once you have a handle on this aspect of building the company, all the other components mentioned earlier can fall neatly and logically into place.

Q: Fair enough. In earlier chats, Po, you emphasized the importance of a customer focus. Are we shifting away from that perspective?

In this case, no. Building a client base before finding and training the right people for your organization makes no sense. It's a mistake that countless organizations have made—that is, spending their initial building energy on lining up clients even before they have located and trained workers to serve those clients.

An analogy might be drawn from the Wild West. No rancher would rustle up thousands of head of cattle and only then begin to look for cowboys (and in our era, cowgirls!) to ride herd over the stampeding animals.

Put another way, you are not ready to attract your first customer until you are prepared to not only satisfy but also to exceed his or her expectations. That can't happen until you have built the right mix and skill set in your employee base. An entrepreneurial service leader is one who can train others to reproduce and scale up highly valued service propositions.

In short, I recommend building people before building a clientele. Let's take things in that order.

Q: Agreed. In your view, what does it mean to "build" a successful employee?

You know that I believe deeply in the power of a highly developed, healthy "POS"—Personal Operating System—for each employee brought into the company. Earlier we discussed some of the specific elements of that Personal Operating System.

Let me expand a little on what a company can do to the build the POS within each of its employees and then I will piggy-back another crucial concept—the PSA or Personal Software Acquisition—onto our discussion of the Personal Operating System.

First, it is folly for any company to presume to instill a sound, responsible Personal Operating System into employees who don't have the basic elements of such a moral system from the first day they enter the organization. No corporate training system that I'm aware of has ever been successful in converting immoral or amoral men and women into caring, responsible, and ethical employees.

This is my way of saying that companies must hire for character from the beginning. The old advice to couples contemplating marriage is "don't expect to change your partner. If you don't like what you have before marriage, you certainly won't like what you have after marriage."

That same central wisdom applies to the hiring process. Someone who lies on their job application will likely fudge their reports and break their word to clients. A virus-laden Personal Operating System within a new hire inevitably brings ever-compounding problems into the company, much like a physical virus can infect not only the entire body but also those with whom it comes in contact.

Q: But certainly companies can nurture and "grow" the Personal Operating Systems of their employees.

Absolutely. In general, I have observed the process working in the following way. Once men and women of sound character have been hired, the culture (or habitat) of the company begins to exert a positive influence to reward a person's moral acts and work ethic and, by contrast, to discourage straying from the path of what Aristotle and Plato called "the Good."

This influence doesn't happen by "rules" posted in an employee lounge or changing area. Instead, it takes place primarily by interaction with respected individuals within the company.

Notice that these individuals don't necessarily have to be at the top of the company food chain. For a new employee, a respected individual might well be a co-worker willing and able to show the newcomer "how things are done" most efficiently and effectively on the job. A similar influential relationship might occur when a co-worker chooses a friendly coaching tone rather than ridicule or "finking to the boss" when a newcomer makes one of the many mistakes that come with being fresh on the job.

The executive and managerial levels can also have a powerful influence on the nurturing and development of each employee's Personal Operating System. Many of these men and women "at the top" assume that their *words*—perhaps in the form of emails, speeches to employee gatherings, or cameos within training videos—are the movers and shakers when it comes to bolstering a healthy POS within employees.

But in truth, language is an increasingly cheap commodity these days. Employees are surrounded by words, words, words from television, radio, cell phones, texting, email, the Internet and other sources by an almost constant blather of language throughout their waking hours. One more written or spoken pep talk or set of wise words from the boss amidst this glut of daily language overload is not going to significantly influence the positive development of an employee's Personal Operating System.

Much more powerful is the employee's impression of what the boss *does*. Virtually every famous moral thinker in Eastern and Western traditions has made this point. As Aristotle put it, "Know the wise man by the way he lives." Employees are conscious of the image and acts of the men and women at the top of their organization.

After all, the day-to-day economic welfare and career future of employees rests largely in the hands of these guiding company leaders. It is of utmost importance, therefore, that company leaders *show* rather than just talk about their own commitment to a healthy Personal Operating System.

Q: What specifics come to mind as ways by which leaders can show that commitment?

In a media age, employees are keenly aware of what causes their company leaders support, what civic projects they support, and what public and professional positions of honor they attain. It comes down to this: to what wheel has my boss put his or her shoulder?

Visible sponsorship of worthwhile public and private initiatives by company leaders is not simply the right thing for privileged individuals to do, nor is it just good "PR" for potential customers. Being sincerely engaged in doing the right thing, however one defines that mission in social terms, sends a powerful message to all employees in the organization. Their own Personal

Operating System becomes energized and enhanced, in other words, by the example of the Personal Operating System of their immediate supervisors, mid- and upper-level managers, and top company executives. Leadership effectiveness and service satisfaction are all built on the foundation of mutual trust, fairness, respect, care, and loyalty.

Q: Some employees would call these influences "pride" in their company and its leaders.

I think that's true. In the same way that waves of good feelings wash over us when we see our country excel at a particular Olympic event, so company employees are inspired by what they see their company doing for others. Their feelings of pride motivate them in large and small ways to "get on the bandwagon" with a company that demonstrates a caring, concerned social consciousness.

The uniform they wear means more to them to the extent that it represents a company doing good things in the world. That pride translates into how employees treat one another, how long they choose to remain employed by the company, and above all how they serve their customers. In a literal sense, employees who feel pride in their association with a great company don't want to let that company down by failing to give excellent service to its clientele. In this way, the individual employee's Personal Operating System is encouraged and sustained by the overall Company Operating System or COS.

Q: It's clear, then, that one way a company can "build" its employees is to keep them perpetually aware and interested in what the company is doing for others. A TV clip of the company chairman on his yacht isn't nearly so influential in this regard as a TV clip of company leaders helping out at a home for the disabled or presenting a company check to a worthy social cause.

Exactly. But building character or the Personal Operating System of each employee isn't the end of the story. The "building" segment of a company's DNA also includes what I call an employee's PSA—Personal Software Acquisition. Going back to our computer analogy, the Personal

Operating System or POS is comparable to the DOS that comprises the basic operational "rules" that determine how well the computer runs.

What the computer is able to *do*, however, is distinct from its DOS. We're all familiar with the additional software we usually need to purchase to make a computer realize its potential in terms of getting work done.

In the same way, building a valuable employee can't stop with the "character + care" piece or POS alone. Well-intentioned, ethical individuals can damage the company enterprise if they don't possess the necessary "software"—that is, the specific skill sets—needed to do their jobs well.

As obvious as this point may seem, we find that it is often ignored throughout business and personal life—and to great expense. Take, for example, the thousands of hours of education to which our children are exposed. Well over 80 percent of that experience is spent listening to instruction in one form or another.

And yet the one skill (or piece of "software") we neglect to provide to our children is how to listen actively, thoughtfully, and strategically. We don't teach them how to pick out the trees from amidst the forest of instruction. They do not know the difference between mere hearing and true listening, even though they will spend most of their academic years in environments where excellent listening skills separate the sheep from the goats.

In another familiar example, consider the communication life of the average business person. In many cases, he or she spends half of each business day on the telephone. Yet no instruction has ever been provided for how to be clear, persuasive, and successful in telephone communications.

We all know people who, through pure ignorance of the impressions they create, are frankly terrible on the telephone. Perhaps they drone on much longer than politeness permits. Or they attempt to convey a list of data that properly should be sent by email or fax, not telephone. Maddeningly, they may take other calls while speaking to us, as if to demonstrate how busy and important they are. Or they may simply be "hard to talk to" because they allow long pauses to fall, making us wonder if they are still on the line or, alternately, "talk our ear off" so that we can't get a word in edgewise.

These are plain but important examples of "software" that is missing in action. Service companies need to decide how they will build the skill capacity of their employees in the same way that we each decide what software we need to load onto our computers.

Admittedly, the whole enterprise of building an excellent employee does begin with a sound POS or Personal Operating System just as a useful computer is grounded in its underlying DOS. But upon that foundation must be built the PSA—Personal Software Acquisition—that converts a well-intentioned individual into a truly effective agent of the company. The Personal Operating System applies just as surely at the leadership level, which is dependent on possessing relevant competencies plus being judged by peers and subordinates as possessing character and care.

Q: Let's talk about a few examples of such "software," as you call it.

I believe that service companies can distinguish two kinds of skill sets or "software" with which to equip their employees: tangible and intangible.

The tangible skill sets vary from service company to service company, depending on the nature of their business. In the case of rather unique start-ups such as the "Geek Squad" in the U.S. (a company that sends computer problem-solvers out to businesses and residences), each employee must have the tangible skills of high-level computer knowledge as well as excellent diagnostic insights and instincts.

At DHL, employees typically had to have well-honed skills in accurate data entry; interpretation of company codes, bills of lading, and scanning techniques; and smart on-the-ground planning skills to maximize the efficiency of their routes.

But equally important in the PSA or Personal Software Acquisition sets of all service employees, no matter what their specific enterprise, are intangible skills. These are harder to train for and are highly dependent on attitude and motivation as well as knowledge (in other words, "wanting" to do it right, not just knowing how to do it right). For example, among the intangible skills crucial to success for a DHL courier are the following:

- Knowing how to be quick about one's job without seeming brusque or impersonal to the client

- Learning to "read" each client to determine what kind of day-to-day working relationship worked best. Did the client have a sense of humor and enjoy some brief banter with the courier? Did the client prefer to remain undisturbed and simply have packages picked up or dropped off without conversation? Did the client have special needs (particularly convenient pick-up times, for example) and was he able to express those needs? (Too often clients expect couriers to be mind-readers.)

- Mastering nonverbal impressions—a sincere smile, a professional appearance, and so forth—that create a good impression for the company and foster further business

- Understanding the role of necessary patience. If the client's place of business is filled with customers, the courier can't assume that "the world stops" when he walks in for a package pickup or delivery. At times even on their busiest days, couriers have to pause, take a deep breath, and wait a moment for the business operator to free himself from customers to sign for a package.

Even though these skills can be taught to some degree in formal company classes, they are probably best learned by guided observation, monitored practice, and eventual independence strengthened by awareness of one's intuitions and confidence in one's insight. This is the "watch me do it, I'll watch you do it, you do it yourself, you teach others to do it" chain of training that has proven so valuable to DHL to this day.

This approach to the learning of intangible skills has the added advantage of building an interdependent, appreciative company culture. Work friendships emerge that make coming to work much more enjoyable than simply showing up as one more stranger among other strangers.

Also engendered by this approach is a "pay it forward" attitude. New employees who have learned from experienced employees take on the responsibility of passing along their knowledge (often with a bit of justified pride in their expertise) to the next generation of new employees in the company. In this way, "what works" gets perpetuated by word of mouth and observation of action instead of by training manuals alone.

Q: So the "building" activity of creating a successful employee is not exclusively top down?

Absolutely not. Any service role in which the employee meets face-to-face with the client inevitably involves a considerable degree of finesse and individual adaptation to the circumstances at hand. No manager at the top—even if he has spent time in the field himself—can know all the tricks of the trade that make a service employee effective with the clients he serves.

Therefore, I want to emphasize the role of respect in management-employee relationships. A manager shows respect to employees by, whenever possible, taking into account their opinions, suggestions, advice, and points of view. If a new procedure or product is being rolled out, a manager would do well to run it by several of his experienced employees in advance to get their take on how it will likely play out with their customers.

Some memorable examples where this kind of on-the-ground knowledge was not solicited would be humorous if they had not proven so economically devastating. Pepsi, for example, gave its European distributors a new line of one-liter plastic soda bottles targeted for retail customers—only to realize (too late) that the average European refrigerator (unlike U.S. refrigerators) did not have a shelf configuration capable of holding the new, tall plastic containers. In a similar gaffe, Chevrolet asked its distribution network throughout Latin and South America to try to market the "Nova"—much to the hilarity of Hispanic customers, for whom "no va" meant "won't go."

The principle is clear: those closest to the customer do have extremely valuable advice, if only managers will respect those they supervise enough to ask for that advice and take it seriously. The three "other" R's hammered home for many of us in elementary school remain true for service sector managers: Respect, Responsibility, and Resourcefulness aren't just words on the blackboard. They are standards by which managers can measure their own performance and that of those they supervise.

Q: Companies sometimes appear to give with one hand while taking away with the other. Do employees fall for such tricks?

Part of the notion of respect is recognizing that your employees are smart. Douglas Macgregor made this point famously in his "Theory Y" management principles: employees by and large are not dumb beasts that need to be driven by the stick of threat and punishment, but instead are thinking, feeling individuals with much to give—if only the company positions itself to receive that input.

In a well-publicized example of apparent double-dealing, Cathay Pacific proposed to share its profits from a very good year by giving cabin crew workers a 4.5 percent salary increase on top of their end-of-year bonuses. The flight attendants union, however, looked at the "fine print" in the proposal only to discover (and make a big noise about) a tricky clause that increased mandatory overtime incrementally each year, resulting in little or no real pay raises for many union members. Cathay Pacific wanted to appear generous in the public eye, but instead came off as somewhat deceitful.

Similarly, a restaurant chain called Café de Coral agreed to increase the salary of staff members to meet new minimum wage laws—but simultaneously (and quietly) cut back the staff's paid lunch-hour break.

In short, respect for one's employees means believing that they are as smart as you are, and resent attempts to "pull the wool over their eyes" just as you would.

Q: *Some leaders are afraid to make that assumption about their employees, fearing that it will give them too much leeway to make damaging mistakes.*

That's where the third R—Resourcefulness—comes into play. Certainly no company should turn its workforce loose half-cocked to do whatever they want in the field. But just as bad are company representatives so unused to making decisions that they find themselves tongue-tied to respond to even the most trivial variation from standard operating procedures requested by their customer.

The happy middle ground, I believe, begins by giving employees access to the resource of instant communication. In this cell phone age, there is no reason why every service representative cannot have near-immediate contact with an "answer-person" near their level of expertise within the company so that the customer's need can be met on the spot instead of days or weeks later, if at all. Mentor-apprentice approaches to learning enable learners to develop competencies while increasing efficacy and self-esteem.

Over time, field representatives gain a sense of their limits with regard to on-the-spot problem solving. To aid in defining this sense of limits, the company can sometimes provide a dollar limit, as many airlines do. Counter clerks at many major airlines, for example, are empowered to make decisions to resolve customer issues up to a total of $100, and thereafter are required to receive supervisor signoff to resolve the problem.

If it is impractical to define dollar limits, a company can encourage resourcefulness on the part of its representatives by educating them (either through classes or by experienced employee-to-inexperienced employee contacts) on permissible and impermissible risks.

In the courier business, for example, an employee needs to know what kinds of on-the-spot decisions and exceptions will cause the overall system to bend a little but not break, versus the kind of decisions and exceptions that cause the system to grind to a halt (requiring a delivery plane, let's say, to take off an hour late). Having this "big picture" view of "what's doable and what isn't" empowers the service employee to help his customer solve local problems whenever possible without bollixing up the carefully designed master system of the company.

Q: There's the old expression, "Physician, heal thyself." Do the same principles that managers apply to their employees also work for managers themselves?

Yes. There's a book I highly recommend: *What Management Is: How It Works and Why It's Everyone's Business,* by Joan Magretta. I was particularly struck by this sentence from the book: "If we want to make smarter choices about our own careers—how we can translate our talents into performance, what we do that causes us to succeed or fail—we need to apply the discipline of management to ourselves."

I'm extrapolating a bit on Magretta's argument, but let me state my position frankly: whatever we as managers propose to do to make our organizations run more smoothly and productively can be equally effective if we apply those principles and strategies to ourselves. There are monetary, spiritual, and well being benefits to thinking about oneself as a personal service business.

I call this concept, "Me, Incorporated." A service leader must fairly and judiciously satisfy his or her own needs in order to optimize his or her ability to lead others well. Speculate with me for a moment on the power that lies in the idea of conceiving of yourself as an organization in need of efficient, effective, and fairly rewarded management. Like a company, you have various "divisions" that compete for limited resources in terms of your time and energy, if not also your money. Often these divisions within oneself are competitive not in a coordinated, constructive way but instead as internal enemies.

Part of me, let's say, wants to improve my tennis game dramatically so that I can shine among my peers at the club. That drive, however, is so strong that I begin to sneak away from obligatory work hours to the point that my professional life suffers. In a word, I am mismanaging the "whole picture" of Me, Incorporated.

To resolve this kind of crisis, we can turn to the tried-and-true economic principle of supply and demand. Analyzed from this perspective, one "division" within the self is making "demands" (more tennis!) at the expense of supply capacity of the rest of the self ("I've got work to do!").

No company can sustain this kind of imbalance for long, nor can the productive self. A company would respond to this kind of dilemma either by increasing its supply to meet the new demand, or acting to trim down the demand to balance with the supply available.

Applied in a personal way to our example, here's how this might work out. We might commit to arriving at work an hour early (with the agreement of our supervisor) in order to literally increase the "supply" of hours available for our use during the day. Further, we might undertake a regimen of diet, exercise, and other healthful practices to increase the supply of energy we have available for both work and non-work activity.

It then becomes possible to meet the increased demands of our tennis ambitions without "ruining the company" (i.e., ourselves), by overtaxing its supply capacity.

Without running through the whole scenario, the reverse case might also be applied: we could become more realistic about our tennis goals and settle to be a good but not great club player for the sake of keeping balance with the demands of our professional life.

Q: The idea of managing oneself as an organization is intriguing. What's another business principle that might apply fruitfully to personal management?

Take the business principle of maximizing one's strengths and minimizing one's vulnerabilities or weaknesses—in other words, focusing on doing what you do best. The field of business mistakes is littered with companies that have boldly diversified into areas they knew too little about, only to return bruised and somewhat wiser to the product or service that made them great in the first place.

Most recently, Cisco Systems made the rueful decision to concentrate again on its main business—computer routers—rather than the variety of personal digital assistants (PDA's) it had tried unsuccessfully to market. MacDonald's, similarly, regularly retreats to its basic menu of inexpensive hamburgers delivered fast when a more complex, expensive array of food choices fails the test of public patronage.

Applied to Me, Incorporated, this principle means soul-searching (the Greek idea of "Know thyself") to the point that you recognize you cannot be "all things to all people." In attempting to do so, in fact, you may be throwing valuable personal energy to the wind, leaving yourself psychically and physically exhausted—and hence less able to do what you do best.

This personal inventory and analysis does not require that you settle monomaniacally on one single skill or occupation. Variety does remain in many ways the spice of life. But it does require a degree of humility in facing up to the fact (as companies must) that you have core areas of strength and passion that must be given their priority, not denied in an effort to play to all crowds at once.

For some managers, this humility involves the admission that "well, I'm really more of a people person than a numbers guy." Notice that the manager in this case has not absolved himself of all involvement with financial data; he simply recognizes that his long-term success will come from exercising and maximizing his people skills rather than knocking his head perpetually against the wall in an effort to compete with financial analysts who love numbers but could care less about people.

Q: How do you know when you have managed "Me, Incorporated" successfully?

Part of that judgment comes from other people, in the form of affection, respect, and trust they accord to you. But the larger part of any assessment of "managing Me" must come from within. I'll call this "psychic payoff" and we will return to the idea later. A well-run "Me, Incorporated" knows at least three things at the end of the day (that being any moment of stock-taking):

- I am doing what I believe I was born to do. My natural skills align well with my ambitions.

- I feel my emotional and physical reserves are in good shape. I have not driven myself to the point of unproductive and harmful exhaustion. I have found my version of the Golden Mean.

- I am justly proud of my day-to-day activities but not conceited about them. I recognize that others may exceed my talents in many ways, but at the same time I feel intuitively that I am giving the best I have, drawn from what I am.

Q: What do you say to the charge that managing "Me, Incorporated" is solipsistic and self-centered?

Managing "Me, Incorporated" is a gift and benefit to those around us, not a display of self-seeking. Even on the family level, who would not rather be around a family member who is balanced, happy, and "comfortable in his own skin," as they say, instead of exhausted, self-conflicted, and depressed? Which would you choose for a spouse, child, or relative?

Those who counsel dysfunctional families, especially when child and spousal abuse are present, consistently give the advice to the abused parent "rescue your family by rescuing yourself"—in other words, put a stop to the abuse you are experiencing as a first step toward ending the abuse that others are experiencing.

That general advice applies admirably to self-management. If we cannot immediately "fix" the local and global problems that surround us, we can at least begin by fixing "Me, Incorporated." Only then do we achieve the emotional, physical, and sometimes financial strength to address the larger problems around us.

We have all heard the sad aphorism, "The slave creates the master." I take that to mean that poorly managed selves—slaves, in effect—end up worsening their condition by their lack of strength to exercise their own power. They give up that power to someone else.

The truth, I believe, is that like any company we each as individuals exist in a context or network of sorts. Our value to that network—in effect, the good that we can do for others—depends directly on how well we have managed "Me, Incorporated."

In return, our ability to survive and thrive is enhanced by the value and support that others in our network can give to us. The relationship, in short, is reciprocal: healthy self-management encourages healthy relationships, and vice versa.

Q: How close do you find the parallel to be between actual business life and the management of "Me, Incorporated"?

Analogies are sometimes dangerous if they imply more falsehoods than the truths they reveal. But I think we can justly catalog three common roles, among many others, in which business life mirrors the management of "Me, Incorporated":

1. The CEO's Office. The CEO is charged with organizing and managing the business of daily life, envisioning what lies ahead for the company, executing the plan, monitoring progress and processes, leading and coordinating the network of staff, and inspiring others to follow. To fulfill these duties, the CEO makes time for personal reflection, conversation and consultation, and decision-oriented meetings. He uses tools such as journals and communication channels. He draws upon resources as broad as ethical systems and as narrow as technical devices.

   Flipped to the management of "Me, Incorporated," you are the owner and top manager of your life—your enterprise, as it were. You are an entrepreneur in the sense that you are living an original life unscripted by anyone else in history. You create the vision for that life and oversee its development and progress. In the process, you reach out to others (resources and "meetings") and welcome these inputs into your eventual life choices.

2. Marketing

   This division of a company is charged with determining the benefits of company services and products for various social sectors and then carrying out campaigns to successfully sell to those groups. The complexities (and, ironically, the simplicities) of this marketing function are captured well in *The 22 Immutable Laws of Marketing*, by Al Ries and Jack Trout.

In a personal management perspective, marketing means becoming aware of what you have to offer ("bring to market") for others. It also involves defining exactly who those "others" are (since no one of us is universally successful in relationships with all people).

Mary Spillane's excellent book, *Branding Yourself: How to Look, Sound, and Behave Your Way to Success,* walks the reader through the specifics of personal marketing. These include your personal honesty and trustworthiness, your ability to be interesting to others, your generosity and kindness, your courtesy, your appropriate professional appearance, and your skill in communicating messages succinctly and persuasively, among other abilities.

The net result of such personal marketing is that you will come to know yourself as a "brand" of sorts—a reliable personal entity recognized for areas of excellence by others.

3. Capital and Asset Management

    It goes without saying that "money matters" influence decisions at all levels within businesses large and small. "Do we want a new computer system?" quickly gets reframed as "Can we afford a new computer system?" "Should we hire an in-house travel manager?" becomes "Can we afford an in-house travel manager." As some executives have admitted, what they knew they *should* do was regularly trumped by what they were told they *could* do by those who controlled the purse strings in the company.

    In personal management, we each have "assets" in the form of material goods as well as biological capacities. We make choices about homes, cars, clothes, electronic devices, vacation travel sometimes wisely and sometimes foolishly. At best, however, we learn from our experience—and can learn even more if we are attuned to the experience of others. A good book in this regard is *Your Money or Your Life*.[15]

Also of help is *Managing Brand Me: How to Build Your Personal Brand*, by Thomas Gad and Anette Rosencreutz (2002). The authors divide their work into stages of personal branding: Developing Brand Me; Integrating Brand Me; Launching Brand Me; Living Brand Me; and Future Brand Me. Without attempting to repeat all the insight tips within this book, let me point you eight guidelines that don't overlap with topics we've already discussed:

- Packaging Brand Me. The authors know that perception is reality when it comes to many business decisions. How you position yourself, even in terms of appearance and references, can dramatically affect your chances for success.

- Setting the Agenda for Brand Me. Enthusiasm for our personal branding can send our minds reeling in all directions. Having a step-by-step (although not inflexible) agenda helps you mark milestones in your accomplishments and measure your progress.

- Go Ahead and Do It for Brand Me. At some point you need to make full commitment to your personal branding venture. An apt analogy is a diver headed off the spring board for a particular challenging dive. There's no half-way. Either you're committed or you're cooked.

- Relationships for Brand Me. Few of us accomplish all we want exclusively by ourselves—and, besides, the encouraging company of supportive friends and colleagues can keep us going through the discouraging times.

- Make a Better Match for Brand Me. The person you brought to the dance isn't necessarily the one you'll leave with. Looking for advantageous alliances is a constant process for personal branding. This does not mean casting off previously helpful friends. As the saying goes, "Make new friends and keep the old; one is silver, the other's gold."

- Give Right Signals to the Market for Brand Me. Don't assume that your target customers can read your mind regarding the products or services you propose to provide. Articulate your offerings, including their benefits. Then articulate them again and again.

- You Are One of a Kind in Brand Me. Of all the authors' insights, this seems to me to be of paramount importance. By thinking of yourself as a unique individual with special abilities, you create a self-fulfilling prophecy: you bring to market unique offerings that can't be found except through you. That's the ultimate payoff of personal branding.

Less obvious than *Brand Me* points but just as vital is our willingness to "manage" our biological assets. To some extent, of course, our physical being manages and monitors itself via the autonomic nervous system (responsible, for example, for controlling heart beat and breathing irrespective of our conscious will).

But large-scale studies of human biology such as the Dartmouth Heart Study[16] demonstrate that each of us can recognize both destructive and constructive health tendencies. In the Dartmouth Heart Study, for example, uncontrolled anger was identified as a prime contributor to heart problems, particularly in men. Doing the right thing by our bodies in terms of rest, nutrition, and exercise is comparable to a facilities maintenance program within a company: you can't run a slum business and you can't exist for long with neglected physical and emotional health.

This point applies especially to managers who attempt to control others by "MGM"—Management by Getting Mad. Emotional explosions at work as a way of motivating or punishing others inevitably backfires to injure the health of the emotional volcano himself. No job pays enough to sacrifice your health and happiness.

KEY POINTS

1. Building any organization begins by building employees with the right character, attitudes, and skills for the organization.

2. Hire for character, train for skills.

3. An individual's Personal Operating System—POS—can be encouraged and enhanced through the influence of respected people. These may be people at any level of authority within the organization.

4. Especially in a media age, what managers show in their actions carries more weight than what they say in influencing the attitudes and behavior of employees.

5. The Company Operating System—COS—can ideally support the development and enrichment of an individual's Personal Operating System (POS).

6. On the foundation of an individual's Personal Operating System (POS) must be built a company-appropriate Personal Software Acquisition (PSA) set of skills, both tangible and intangible.

7. A best first step for a manager seeking to build an effective work team is to show respect (through active listening, idea solicitation, and appreciation) for the individuals he supervises.

8. Employees gain power to solve local problems through Resourcefulness, made possible by meaningful resources employees can access quickly and reliably.

9. Core concepts for best practices in managing organizations can be fruitfully applied to "Me, Incorporated"—that is, the kind of disciplined self-management that leads to psychic wealth, improved performance, and enhanced relationships.

Chapter Five

Articulate: the Heart of Branding

Q: The moment of truth for service companies, or any organization, probably comes when they unveil themselves to their target clientele and to the public generally.

This moment is simultaneously thrilling and frightening. All the hard work that has gone into understanding one's business, designing viable strategies, and building a workforce is put to the test in the first hours, days, and weeks of "articulation"—that is, saying clearly and powerfully who you are and what you propose to do for your clients.

The thrill comes from seeing the company leap into reality as a player in business and society. The fright comes from our natural fear of making mistakes in our first, crucial debut.

We know that, like a first date in our social life, "first impressions matter." If things go well, they set the stage for all the positive developments that can follow. If the initial debut is an ill-conceived flop, it's hard to undo the damage.

Q: Not to dwell on the negative, but say a bit more about what you mean by a "flop."

Poorly planned or executed company debuts (or debuts of new products or services from existing companies) typically go astray in one or more of these three ways. First, the debut can be so lacking in distinguishing features or originality that is "fades into the light of common day," in the words of the poet Wordsworth, like stars disappearing at daylight.

I'm not arguing here for spectacularism, in which new companies do absurd things simply to catch the public eye. But there must be a compelling proposition, "something new or better," in the appearance, potential, or story of the new venture sufficient to compete with all the other media claims on the attention of the public.

Second, debuts often fail because they fall into the rut of "me too" presentation. For example, countless entrepreneurs, having observed the success of Coca Cola and Pepsi around the world, have attempted to produce their own line of cola. But you've never heard of these many attempts because their product launch fell in line behind the giants in the soft-drink industry and became lost in their shadow.

Finally, debuts flop because they are "all sizzle and no steak"—that is, they are long on expressions of excitement and short on a clear statement of customer benefits.

We have all had the experience of watching a TV commercial and then saying to ourselves or someone else in the room, "I just don't get it." The commercial misfired not because it failed to attract our attention, but instead because it failed to *do* anything with our attention. It never moved us along from initial curiosity to solid brand perception, about which we will have much to say in a moment.

Q: We probably should set aside the "how" of articulating the nature and benefits of a company until we discuss the "what" and "why." What should a company consider in shaping its articulation for the world to see and hear, and why are these components important to the success of the company's debut?

Let's start with the "what" question. Thomas Gad wrote a fine book titled *4-D Branding* (referenced in the Resources section) which inspired me to extend the list of aspects of brand articulation to twelve in my own terms from his initial formulation of four.

First, a company must articulate its *function*. Put simply, the customer just wants to know "what can you do for me?" Any print ad, speech, or TV/radio spot that does not answer this question is doomed to failure. The statement of a company's function can be covert rather than overt so long as it is powerful and thoroughly perceived by its audience.

A new perfume company, for example, may not spell out in words that "our product makes you smell good"—but the alluring use of sensual images in its magazine ads communicates persuasively that one's attractiveness to others and sense of personal beauty will be enhanced by purchase of the new product.

An important part of articulating function involves backing up your claims with proof that you can do the job. For a travel agency, this may involve assurances about the company's knowledge base: "We know Australia like no one else!" A bank may focus on its benchmarking against competitors, "earning the highest returns in the industry." A contractor may point to his stability: "Family-owned and family-run since 1981."

In these and other ways, companies increase the likelihood that the potential customer will believe the articulation of function—or at least give it enough credit to look into the company more thoroughly and perhaps give it a try.

Second, a company must articulate its mental advantage. Sometimes this aspect of articulation is directed externally, as when a new computer company features interviews with its cutting-edge programmers or visionary leaders like the late Steve Jobs.

Just as often, however, the articulation of mental advantage is an internal "gut check"—an honest examination of where the new venture stands in relation to the intellectual level of its competitors. As one Silicon Valley executive put it, "The big-name firms can out-do us, but they can't out-know us." So long as knowledge is power, superiority in knowledge (no matter what the field) will likely bring market advantage.

A company can evaluate its mental advantage not only by reviewing the qualifications of its employee "brain trust." The company can also examine its unique intellectual capital in the form of proprietary formulas and techniques, patents, trademarks, copyrights, and exclusive partnerships with other sources of valuable industry knowledge.

It can also determine what professional conferences its employees are attending and what they contributed at these meetings. Were they just listeners in the back row? Or did others in the industry come to hear the latest research and development news from your people?

This kind of mental evaluation can assure a company that "we're not all fluff," but instead have significant ideas and methods that can be mined to produce improved products and services, with the market rewards that flow from such improvements.

Third, a company should assess and articulate its social attributes. Not every employee of the company has the gift to be a social star, but each of these individuals can learn how to be "good company"—the kind of people others look forward to seeing, want to be around, and introduce as friends rather than professional acquaintances.

The vital lesson learned best by experience is that the business world is and has always been a "people world"—that is, a domain where deals happen and networks emerge because the people involved have an appropriate sense of humor, a sincere concern for one another, and decency about them that attracts the trust and respect of others.

In articulating who they are and what they do, therefore, a company cannot ignore the social dimension. Checklist questions along this line are obvious: Do our people project a friendly, approachable image? Do our managers and executives have the social skills to "work a room" in order to meet and get to know others? Do customers sense that our representatives are patient, generous with their time, and genuinely courteous in their interactions (including to the lowliest receptionist)? Do our public spokespeople perform well in media interviews, portraying the company as an enjoyable, energized place of business?

Fourth, a company should appraise and articulate its dominant emotional dimension. Of course, we all have our good days and bad days in terms of feelings and moods. But seen from 30,000 feet, so to speak, what can be said about the general emotional climate of the company?

Is it a place where pessimism and sarcasm are the primary modes of interpersonal communication? Where people expect chaos and confusion, then cynically joke about it when things go wrong? Or—we hope—is the work environment one in which people are enthused by what they are working on, find it easy to share a smile with co-workers, and look forward to getting to the office or into the field most days?

Companies can refine their evaluation of corporate "EQ"—Emotional Quotient—by estimating the number of emotion givers versus emotion takers in the firm. An emotion giver is a person whose emotions prove contagious for those around them (for better or worse).

A group leader, for example, has the opportunity to be an emotion giver by setting the emotional tone of a meeting, interview, or hallway conversation. He or she can be sincerely upbeat and optimistic, and thereby positively influence the attitudes, behavior, and productivity of the group. Or the group leader can bring his or her emotional "baggage" to work, allowing some upset in personal life to cloud interactions and relationships in the workplace.

An emotion taker, by contrast, is one who, chameleon-like, allows his or her emotions to be colored by those who are more emotionally dominant at work. A secretary, for example, may be prone to taking emotional cues from his or her boss each day. If the boss is angry or depressed, the emotion-taking secretary will tend to imitate those feelings and spread them to others during the workday.

Frankly, training departments in organizations do not usually do enough in the area of emotional understanding and training.

Granted that few company trainers want to take on the responsibility of in-depth psychological counseling. But they should be ready to make individual employees aware of how their emotions are being perceived by others, what effect they are having on the general emotional climate of the company, and how those emotions influence productivity and worklife satisfaction. In short, training departments are often too focused on skill development rather than personal insight development.

Fifth, a company must weigh and articulate its moral dimension. Any discussion of morality stands in danger of becoming abstruse and foggy— "where the rubber meets the sky," as one wit put it.

Let me be very clear about what professional morality means to me: Does a person know what ethical obligations he owes to the company and does that person also know what ethical obligations he owes to fellow employees and team members, the customer, the public, and the environment? Moreover, if these ethical obligations conflict (as they sometimes do), does the person know how to use a variety of resources (inside and outside the company) to find an ethical resolution to the conflict?

An example of this kind of ethical conflict could be as follows: An employee is ethically bound by loyalty to his company not to reveal proprietary or sensitive in-house information that might adversely affect the company. But if the employee becomes knowledgeable about some company misdeed (let's say a bad batch of baby formula) that has the potential to harm others, the employee is also ethically bound to do the right thing as a human being, not just as an employee.

The resources he might turn to in order to resolve this ethical dilemma include using the "whistle-blowing" mechanisms most companies have put in place so that employees can report significant problems without fear of retribution and without having to call newspaper and TV reporters.

A company's moral commitments—those it lives by, not just prints in the annual report—are its trust bond with customers and the public. The specifics of these commitments can be formulated as simply as the *li* of Confucian teaching, the Ten Commandments of the Judaeo-Christian tradition, or any other rather common-sense statements of how human beings should ideally interact.

No company or individual employee is perfect in this regard, of course. The point is that the company *knows* its ethical standards, *aspires* to achieve them, and *repairs* incidents in which company morality has been compromised. In specific terms, the company constantly strives to hire at all levels for character and caring. Lacking these qualities, a employee will not find success in a service business.

In the biological analogies we've used often so far in our conversation, the company has to be on guard against moral viruses, just as we watch for the first symptoms of illness in our personal health. We don't wait for viral pneumonia to take us right up to death's door. We hurry to our physician to treat the problem in its earliest stages. Similarly, a company should intercept moral viruses in their infancy, not when they have gained a powerful foothold within the firm.

Take the simple matter of "white lies," for example. A major U.S. car company in 2010 decided to give bonuses to its salespeople based on survey results (1 to 10, with 10 being best) from their customers.

Eager to get these bonuses, many of the salespeople told each of their customers that they needed straight 10's on the customer survey form, and that if the customer didn't feel he or she could give straight 10's, the salesperson wanted a chance to repair any performance area less than a 10 or would simply ask the customer not to complete the survey.

As a result, more than half of the entire salesforce received straight 10s on their year's worth of survey results from customers. Befuddled by this statistically unlikely result, company executives fanned out to interview salespeople, asking them if they had unduly influenced customers in any way to give them straight 10s on the survey form. The great majority of salespeople denied even discussing the survey form with customers.

Rather than call hundreds of their salespeople liars, the car company abandoned the bonus program entirely, much to the consternation of the sales force.

This is a clear case where fudging the ethical assumptions underlying a customer survey proved to be a lose-lose for the company and its salespeople. A moral virus had somehow convinced a few salespeople at first, and many later on, that it was somehow OK to skew the results of a customer survey by guiding the customer's responses in a manipulative way.

Had the company discovered the virus early on (as it could have by reviewing early survey results) it could have wiped it out by making each salesperson very aware of the company ax that would fall on anyone gaming the system.

When others see that the company won't stand for relatively mild immoralities (such as telling a customer a fib about a delayed delivery ("the truck broke down") or an incorrect price quote ("the computers are acting up today"), the virus of unethical behavior can be nipped in the bud. Small immoralities don't magnify and spread to large, company-wide deceptions (as occurred notoriously in the cases of Enron, Countrywide Financial, and other "problem" companies). To sum up this point, the design of a service proposition or organization should consider the implications of its operations, service propositions, and service failures at three levels of morality: effects on individuals, groups, and systems.

A good test for one's reaction to moral viruses is to ask yourself how you would feel if a family member or close friend looked you in the eye and told you a bald-faced lie, such as "I can't come to your anniversary party because my boss is sending me on a business trip."

When you later discover that there was no such business trip, you can't help but feel a corroding effect on your relationship with the person in question.

Q: Why do so many people turn to fibs and white lies as a regular part of their professional lives?

Well, these small immoralities or viruses may get the person "off the hook" of some awkward dilemma for the moment. But in the long run, being successful at small lies simply tempts a person to become more and more adept at large lies—until the roof caves in and he is caught in his web of deceit.

Sometimes employees defend their small lies by saying, "If I told the truth to the customer, it would have made the company look bad." That's where a clear-thinking manager has to step in to turn the employee's moral head around.

The company is far better served by honesty than by deception. In the case of a late delivery, it's much better to tell the truth—"I don't know why that shipment is late, but I'll find out and call you right back"—than to fabricate a story out of thin air. This point applies equally to company leaders. Moral viruses in one's Personal Operating System negatively influence judgments about one's quality of service leadership and the positive or negative effects that result from that leadership.

Q: We were halfway through your list of twelve dimensions necessary for the full articulation of a company's nature and goals.

The sixth dimension of articulation, and perhaps the hardest to talk about, is the spiritual aspect of professional life. By "spiritual" I do not mean a particular religion, doctrine, or theology.

Instead, I have in mind a definition along these lines: being aware of and awake to the world all around you, including its problems and injustices. For example, does your company have a corporate social responsibility (CSR) policy that translates into action on behalf of local and global issues such as decimation of rain forests, approaching extinction of certain plants and animals, and oppression of disempowered human beings?

Articulating these concerns may not contribute immediately to company profits. But taking a stand for what's right whether in your own area or internationally is an act on behalf of the human spirit we share across borders and traditions.

To be clear, I don't view companies as political action committees. But neither do I see them as spiritually neutral organizations that can ignore the larger forces shaping their world. Being "spiritual" as a company simply means caring about people and things beyond yourself.

Seventh, companies should also articulate their relative wealth. Hedge fund managers do so regularly by disclosing to potential customers the total amount they have under their control. Banks attract clients by advertising they are "$50 billion strong" or some similar claim.

Although statements about wealth can be misused as crude bragging, they can also be positively framed as assertions that invite confidence and new business. One start-up company in the United States used this positive approach by revealing that famed investment guru Warren Buffet had invested $400 million in the company.

Other entrepreneurial ventures may refer to the specific venture capital firm that gave them first- or second-round funding, with the clear message that a careful and prestigious venture capital group found the new business worthy of their investment.

Wealth is not a guarantee of morality in business dealings or proof of professional expertise. But it does provide additional evidence one can use when deciding where to place trust, particularly in new business undertakings.

Q: That may all be true, but what can a new company do if it has little wealth?

That's the condition of most new companies—long on talent and short on cash. In that case, a company should point to its trend lines rather than its bank account. A new firm lacking substantial cash might, for example, make the point that its business is increasing by 20 percent each quarter.

124

Those kinds of statements, so long as they are accurate, encourage customers in the belief that they are "going with a winner" rather than hitching up to a business that will soon fail.

Q: *And the eighth dimension of articulation?*

Companies must take a stand on the physical health of their employees—all of them—as well as the influence of their products and services on public health. The old saying goes that "we spend our health getting wealthy, and then our wealth trying to get healthy."

In many countries, people spend more than half of all their life's healthcare dollars in the last two weeks of their life.

While companies have every right to expect an honest day's work for an honest day's pay, no company gains anything by working its employees beyond the limits of good health. The American Management Association estimates that it costs a company about one year's pay to replace a mid-level manager, when recruiting, interviewing, selection, and training costs are all summed up.

So for financial reasons alone (and of course moral reasons as well), companies need to articulate and act on their position on employee health.

Some firms do so by installing company gyms and making time available for employees to use them regularly. Other companies have "quit smoking" campaigns and a variety of assistance programs for everything from anger management to substance abuse.

And ninth on our list of points for company articulation is leadership within the tribe. The word "tribe" may sound somewhat primitive to apply to modern organizations. But I use the word in the sense defined by Seth Godin in his book, *Tribes: We Need You to Lead Us*: "a tribe is a group of people, large or small, who are connected to one another, to a leader, and to an idea."

Notice in this regard that a tribe differs from a crowd, which is merely a leaderless group usually lacking in a dominant or unifying idea. A tribe also differs from a network in that the latter branches out laterally, usually without hierarchy, while the former involves a complex pyramid of roles, each with their own duties and relation to tribal traditions.

Companies need to articulate their tribal nature so that all employees confront and answer the loyalty question: do I or don't I "belong" to this company in terms of my professional commitments and best efforts?

This issue is particularly important in managing so-called "Millennial" workers (those born after 1982). If research on this group is to be believed, a significant segment of Millennials feel identification to a skill-set or occupation ("I'm a programmer and right now I'm working for Microsoft") rather than to a company.

When employees think of themselves as interlopers or somehow "on loan" to a company rather than truly belonging to the company tribe, it's no surprise when they change jobs often, give lackluster performance, and constantly have their resumes out with headhunters.

Nor do they give much credence or respect to the tribal leader, whether in the form of their group supervisor or an upper-level manager or CEO. After all, they do not consider this individual "their" leader, since they haven't fully signed on as members of his or her tribe.

Thankfully, many companies have overcome this "dysfunctional tribe" syndrome by carefully aligning job responsibilities with the talents and work preferences of individual employees. When you like your job, it's hard not to become part of the team or tribe—and harder yet to quit a good thing to earn a little more elsewhere.

One especially effective way to draw employees deeper into the team or tribe mentality is to distribute leadership responsibilities generously. Leadership behaviors don't take place only at the top echelons of progressive service companies.

At DHL, whether the employee at hand is a courier delivering documents, a frontline salesperson, or a backroom shipping clerk, each has opportunities to exert leadership on a regular basis by recognizing problems and taking the lead in solving them. This exercise of creative abilities pays dividends to the company (by resolving problems before they fester) and to the individual by building his or her self-esteem and giving the person confidence to rise within the company.

Mutual trust, fairness, respect, care, and loyalty promote the development and maintenance of positive and productive social relationships at all levels of business.

Q: And your final few items on the list of twelve?

Companies must articulate their expectations for the visual dimension of business experience. In the 1960s we may have lived through or at least read about an "anything goes" approach to personal appearance.

Believe me, the 60s are over! Malcolm Levene's excellent book, *10 Steps to Fashion Freedom*, and other so-called "dress for success" books universally make the point that we are each judged by others on how we appear, not just what we say or do.

This assertion does not mean that a "power suit" (whether for a professional man or woman) is always the right choice for any business occasion. In fact, comfortable "corporate casual" clothing is often a much better option for many business situations and audiences.

But the central point remains: one's visual appearance, including being reasonably fit and well-groomed, cannot be denied as an influential aspect of who gets the deal, who gets interviewed, who gets hired—and, for that matter, who gets fired.

I don't dispute that a book can't be judged by its cover, and no sensible businessperson would ever base a business relationship exclusively on someone's visual appearance. But book covers do guide the hand when we browse in a bookstore. Appropriate, attractive visual appearance not only creates a good initial impression but also reassures the customer throughout the business relationship that you respect him or her and want to represent your company professionally. The point is that strategic thinking and planning can be used to design, create, develop and improve an attractive personal impression that encourages a productive business relationship.

Eleventh on my list for company articulation is a commitment on the part of each employee to personal and professional growth. Many organizations use the phrases "lifelong learning" and "continuous improvement" for this kind of engagement. To take the negative attitude, "I'm hired, now I can kick back," is not only damaging to the career of the person involved but also to all those who observe or work with that person. For each of us, lifelong learning and continuous improvement require an effort to understand workplace and industry events, opportunities, obstacles, and relationships, and then to grow from such knowledge in terms of one's actions and attitudes.

Finally, company articulation depends on the overarching quality of character for all employees and for the organization itself. Companies including DHL do well to "hire for character," since it is usually difficult and often impossible to instill positive character traits in those who lack them when they come aboard as new employees. We recognize character in a holistic way—an impression we form of an individual, a group, or a company typically in the very early stages of our interaction with them. Drawing on our own intuitions, insights, and human experience, we are usually quick to identify those who consistently strive to do the right things, the right way, at the right time, and for the right reasons. We tend to relate well to these individuals, groups, or organizations—and want to do business with them—because we trust them. The overall importance of sound character to personal and business success should never be underestimated.

1. Articulation goes far beyond naming the company or putting up a neon sign. Articulating the nature and goals of one's company involves a top-to-bottom evaluation of all the main factors that contribute to the company brand and identity.

2. Companies often miss opportunities for clear articulation of who they are and what they do by obscuring their distinguishing features, playing the "me too" game by falling in line behind market leaders, and failing to define the specific benefits they offer to potential customers.

3. To achieve fully-considered articulation of their essence and brand, companies must specify their function in unmistakable and customer-relevant terms: what does the company do and how will it benefit me, the customer?

4. Companies should also articulate their mental edge or advantage—the "intellectual property" and capacity they bring to the competitive marketplace.

5. Companies should articulate their social attributes, emphasizing the kinds of attitudes and behaviors they want all their employees to display inside and outside the company.

6. Companies should articulate the appropriate roles of emotion within their organizations. The EQ or Emotional Quotient of company representatives is as important in business terms as their IQs.

7. Companies should articulate their moral positions—and then turn those assertions into day-to-day reality through effective training programs, careful monitoring, and quick response to moral infractions.

8. Companies should articulate and exercise their corporate social responsibility (CSR), demonstrating that they care about the larger world in which they do business.

9. Companies should articulate their wealth status (or path to wealth) in an appropriate way that does not come off as bragging. Wealth, rightly described, can be a strong component in attracting new clients and retaining the confidence of existing clients.

10. Companies should articulate their position on measures to support healthy lifestyles and workstyles for their employees (their main asset).

11. Companies should articulate the importance of tribal membership and shared leadership. Employees should never feel they are "on loan" to the company but are not true members of its community or tribe.

12. Through lifelong learning and continuous improvement, all members of a company can "up their game" in terms of professional performance and personal job satisfaction.

13. Character, a quality that companies should seek out and evaluate carefully at the time of hiring, is a deep-seated inclination and commitment on the part of individuals, groups, and the organization itself to strive to do the right things, the right way, at the right time, and for the right reasons.

Chapter Six

Operate: The Art of Decentralizing Authority

Q: At this point we've worked our way through the stages you have termed Understand, Design, Build, and Articulate. One would suspect at the end of this string would come that popular corporate word, "Execute." You chose "Operate" instead.

Given the terminations and layoffs in virtually all industries these days, "execute" may have an unintended and dark meaning for many employees! More seriously, I purposely chose the word "operate" based on its oldest root meaning, according to the Oxford English Dictionary: "to take pains, to exert, to labor." This sense of the word is still maintained in the medical connotations of "having an operation."

I want to emphasize by the word "operate" that the day-to-day work of running even the best-designed service company, or any business for that matter, involves exertion and occasional moments when one's labor is painful.

The analogy of labor prior to child-birth is appropriate here. Company leaders at all levels experience "labor pains" in their efforts to bring new life into the company and nurture what they have already spawned. My point is that organizational leadership is no joy-ride. The professional lives of thousands of men and women—and by extension their families—are in your hands.

By contrast, "execute" sounds so clinical and technical to me—something that connotes the flipping of switches and issuance of commands rather than the hard, complex tasks involved in working with real people.

Q: Viewed from the outside, a company like DHL would seem to be a well-tuned engine where every cog simply has to perform its limited function.

You said it well: "viewed from the outside." I had the responsibility and privilege over several decades to view the DHL operation from the inside. I assure you that the real workings of the company were not automatic, robotic, or cog-like, even though individuals did have coordinated job descriptions that added up to successful performance.

The "cog" analogy doesn't fit DHL, or service businesses generally, because it presumes a machine-like predictability about daily worklife. That just isn't the case for service businesses. We know we operate in a larger company context, but at the same time we have to use our individual smarts, intuitions, and insights to make countless adjustments, adaptations, exceptions, and alterations if our role in the total company picture is to be successful.

Q: We will withdraw the word "cog" from discussion—but offer a better concept in its place.

This may sound a bit artsy, but I believe it to my core: every employee in companies that are moving forward is a conductor of sorts. Before him or her appear the wide range of instruments in the form of customers, co-workers, supervisors, prospective clients, business partners, community members, down to the local traffic cop.

The goal of the conductor is to make music instead of cacophony from this range of instruments. Some are out of tune, so to speak—they need special attention to bring them into harmony with the rest of the group. Other parts of this orchestra are too loud (perhaps in their unreasonable demands or angry manner), while others are too soft, the "silent majority" who do have thoughts and feelings that need to be drawn out, if a company is ever going to truly understand its clientele.

Through exquisitely attuned sensing and moment-by-moment adaptations, the conductor/employee does his or her best to bring all these players together into an ensemble that fits the company mission or "score."

Q: That's an engaging thought and certainly more humanistic than picturing ourselves as cogs—oops, the word occurred again. But aren't you setting yourself an almost impossible task in finding these "conductor" individuals?

Not really. The function of wise hiring for any firm should be to base selection on character and capacity. The presence of sound character— something that probably can't be taught within the time-line and resources of most companies—assures the firm that its new hires will knit well with the ethical fabric of the organization.

The presence of capacity—and here's where the "conductor" potential comes in—gives the company the realistic hope that the new hire will grow into his or her job. Better yet, the company wants that individual to grow out of the job—that is, to master one level of performance within the company as preparation for increased areas of responsibility.

Placing such conductors strategically becomes of paramount importance for a global company. Distributed models of leadership are a critical component of long-distance service value chains and global service networks.

Q: So you're hiring individuals with the talent to be conductor/employees, even though they may not have already achieved those skills or experiences in their job history elsewhere?

Precisely. Once brought aboard at DHL, it was our "program" to give new hires incremental opportunities to conduct a larger and more challenging ensemble of players.

We did so in three steps. First, we pushed decision-making to the lowest level.

Q: Stop there for a moment. Specifically what do you mean?

Picture one hundred clients, all of whom want their packages picked up or delivered "right away." No executive in the company can get on the phone with either the courier or the customers to orchestrate the most efficient, effective path for making these pickups and deliveries happen to the satisfaction of all concerned.

The decision is actually too complex for computers, which would at best give a mapquest-like route for the straightest line between the various points of business service.

Pushing decisions to the lowest level meant relying on the intelligence of the courier to surpass that of any computer. No software program, after all, can meaningfully factor in the feelings, pressures, daily schedule changes, and personal preferences of even one hundred customers.

The courier has to have the individual smarts to know when to "go out of his way" to help out a customer in a time-crunch situation and, for that matter, when not to let a customer's demands get out of hand. Again, the goal for the company and the conductor/employee was to make music out of the day's work, not noise. Driving decisions downward to smart, in-the-field employees was crucial in our efforts to serve our client base and build market share.

Q: You mentioned three steps before I interrupted.

The second step was teaching strategic thinking at all levels. Too often "strategy" is the work of men and women on the top floors of company headquarters. Once formulated, it gets sent down, like Moses bearing the Ten Commandments down from Mt. Sinai, to the troops who are expected to carry out the strategy.

This way of conceiving of strategic thinking directly short-circuits our first notion of each employee as a conductor and decision-maker. Although there will always be decisions and policies "from the top" in any organization, there will also be important choices, options, and alternatives weighed and selected by those at the middle and bottom of the company.

Q: What do you mean by "teaching" strategic thinking? Is this a matter of bringing people into a training center for formal classes of some kind?

In some companies, yes. At DHL, our "classes" tended to occur in the field and one-on-one or one-to-a-small-group rather than in a classroom setting. The great majority of these teaching moments were Socratic in nature.

The experienced, successful DHL employee would pose nonjudgmental "why" questions to the newbie employee: Why did you take an extra couple minutes to talk with Mrs. Fu about her shipping needs for next week instead of just picking up her package for today? Why did you re-arrange your usual route to help Acme Accounting meet its filing deadlines in the U.S.?

Just as often, the answers to these questions weren't verbal at all. The inexperienced employee was given the chance to see strategic thinking in action by observing the choices and decisions made by the experienced, successful employee. The "ah ha" moment for the new employee often came when he or she saw the common sense (or uncommon sensibility) in the experienced employee's strategy. Everyday, every human being experiences opportunities to improve his or her leadership quality and effectiveness.

Q: Didn't this approach encourage a "copy cat" culture?

Not at all. The goal was not to imitate exactly what the experienced employee did, but rather to grasp why that employee made those decisions. Teaching strategic thinking at all levels comes down to building an in-depth understanding of possible choices that can be made in various situations.

That's the "why" of strategy. The exact choice made on the basis of such understanding depends on the individual employee and the circumstances at hand.

Q: But surely a lot of mistakes were made on the path to wise strategy.

Of course. At DHL, and a host of other successful companies in all sectors, the question is not whether a mistake was made but rather what was done after the mistake occurred. There's a natural human tendency, I suppose, to flaunt what we've done well and hide what we've done poorly.

We tried to fight that unproductive approach at DHL. A mistake, we felt, was similar to a pothole in the pavement: mark it and tell everyone about it so that they don't have the same mishap you did. In this way, a mistake became an opportunity for corporate learning.

Physicians, by the way, are assiduous in studying not just the surgical or therapeutic techniques that led to positive outcomes, but also the attempts that failed. They are as interested in medical interventions and trials that didn't work as they are in those that did—and they fill their medical journals with the annals of both medical successes and failures.

That's what "blind studies" in the scientific method are all about: we're trying to locate the contrast between the usual ways—the ways pockmarked by mistakes—and better ways. If we ignore mistakes or, worse, make an effort to hide them from others, we end up repeating those mistakes expensively and unintelligently.

Q: When employees are put more and more into the challenging and strategic role of conductor, do they react with enthusiasm or resistance?

You are raising a vital issue: the watershed between those who want to learn and those who only want to earn. DHL never presented itself to new employees as a work haven where they could plod along until retirement.

The model was much more that of an elevator. No matter at which "floor" they got on the company elevator, our expectation was that they were on their way up. When occasional employees metaphorically flipped the "stop" button on the elevator and indicated that they didn't want to go higher (or preferred to sink lower in terms of responsibilities), we acted swiftly to replace them. An employee's resistance to new learning (or rising on the elevator) was infinitely more indicting, we felt, that any single mistake he or she could have made during the work day.

In this regard, leaders have to model the way toward a willingness to learn. Judgments followers make about a leader's character and caring disposition influence their judgments about the leader's effectiveness—and the degree to which they, as employees, want to "follow the leader."

Q: You've managed countless hundreds of individuals on the upward elevator toward increased organizational responsibility. Does one person stand out in your memory as an example of the three principles you've described?

I could spend the rest of the day telling you about men and women who have literally bloomed before my eyes as professionals once they were uplifted by the nurturing forces of trust in their intelligence, a focus on strategic thinking and a learning approach to mistakes.

But let me briefly recount the experience of my former Hong Kong office manager, Andy Tseng. In spite of the temptation at upper levels of the company to micromanage and second-guess his leadership, DHL took the courageous step of turning over to Andy the authority and discretion he needed to make virtually every decision for the successful operation and expansion of the local branch.

In a demonstration of confidence that most companies would find rare indeed, Andy drew up a business plan and budget that within a short amount of time were agreed to and signed off by John Kerr, our Regional Managing Director for the Far East. From that point on, Andy was steering the bus. He proceeded with his plan without interference or arm-chair quarterbacking from upper levels of authority in the company.

To say that Andy's business efforts proved successful would be a vast understatement. But even more important was what this approach to management did for Andy as an employee and prime contributor to DHL. He felt that he was DHL for Hong Kong, not that he merely worked for DHL.

He experienced job satisfaction by bringing his dreams to reality—job satisfaction that pay raises or other incentives could never equal. Andy's energy and enthusiasm became legendary not only in Hong Kong but throughout the company. In short, others saw in Andy what they too could become. You can't ask for more from a manager.

Q: Much has been written in the leadership literature about "empowerment." Is that what DHL promoted, as illustrated in Andy's case?

I resist the concept of "empowerment" simply because it often implies a complete transfer of power to employees instead of a partnership of responsibility. I like the term "decentralized authority."

Andy at all times knew that he operated the Hong Kong branch within the web, culture, and habitat of the larger DHL world. He was not "empowered" in the sense of being divorced from the counsel and support of his mentors and upper level managers, including myself. Instead, Andy experienced a significant amount of authority (but not total authority) being conferred upon him—and that demonstration of confidence on the part of the company proved transformative for the better in Andy's remarkable professional life.

Q: What advice would you have for companies seeking to decentralize authority in the ways you have described?

Do so a step at a time. Even the most capable employees can be overwhelmed by too much responsibility given all at once. It's better to dole out increasingly independent decisions and judgments, then work in a mentoring fashion to assess how those experiences played out—and what new challenges might be appropriate for the employee's growth and usefulness to the company.

We used the concept of "stretching" to describe this process of growth. And like all stretching, sometimes the results are painful the next morning, at least for a while. I recall one of our airport supervisors who was doing well on his upward growth curve within the company.

But on a given day, he faced a decision he wasn't ready for: he had to decide on the spot to leave some courier bags behind from the flight for which they were scheduled. The aircraft operator told him there just wasn't enough space to fit all the bags. He was told he either had to take all the bags off the aircraft and wait for the next available flight, or sacrifice the prompt and expected delivery time of a few of the bags.

The gravity of this kind of situation in the courier industry is not trivial. Huge real estate, stock, and other business transactions may depend on receiving documents and other business materials exactly when promised. A day late in many cases simply won't do. Our airport supervisor in this circumstance literally held the reputation of the company in his hands.

What did he decide? In a way, it didn't matter: he was stuck with a Hobson's choice in which neither alternative was acceptable. What he learned from this experience—and told many others in the company about--was to scan the larger environment for possible solutions, not to crash head-on into last-minute decision-making.

He reflected on whether he could have built stronger friendships with the airline staff—friendships which could have motivated the aircraft operator to help him find solutions that were a bit "outside the box." He also pondered the levels at which he could have made these friendships with those upon whom he depended at the aircraft company.

I call this the "doorman approach." Each employee, including the supervisor in this example, needs to take seriously the potential influence of good relations with everyone who passes through the "door" of his daily professional life, no matter what that person's relative status or importance. A first-year customs officer who has been treated with courtesy and good humor may turn out to be as valuable in some stressful situations as the Minister of Communications and Transportation of a country.

As the saying goes, it is still a "people world." Good relationships motivate all of us to do things for others that may stretch our convenience or the strict interpretation of the rulebook a bit. The point for this supervisor is that those relationships needed to be in place prior to his emergency. Building bridges to other helpful people in one's profession should happen before the flood, not after.

Q: In the way you describe decentralizing authority and encouraging individual employee initiative, the word "manager" seems somehow out of kilter. Doesn't the word "manager" contradict some of the concepts of decentralized authority?

In a word, yes. The word "manager" harkens back to an earlier industrial age where untrained, largely unskilled workers (often termed "the rabble") were told what to do and then monitored by an authority figure who had no interest in giving up an iota of his power over them.

If I could rewrite business history, I would insert the word "entrepreneur" or, for inside-the-company operations, "intrapreneur" instead of manager. Both of these terms convey the importance of creativity, experimentation, and risk-taking that is missing from traditional associations connected with "manager." The overarching goal for any management scheme in service companies is for distributed models of leadership to promote and enable front-line service workers to deliver individualized personal service—the kind of service that communicates to the client, "I care about you and I care about doing my job right."

Q: But both "entrepreneur" and "intrapreneur" sound like relatively lonely self-starters. How does that square with your thoughts about building a company culture where social interaction, learning and relationships are paramount?

Earlier I remarked that strategy in a company can be taught. Let me amend that statement, just to play with words and ideas for a moment, to "caught" instead of "taught."

At DHL, we hardly ever lectured our fast-track supervisors. Instead, we put them in an environment (on a budget team, for example) where they quickly became caught up in seeing the big picture, then making the appropriate business decision that supported that big picture.

You know that I love fish and come from an ancestry of fishermen. Showing others the big picture of a company is like lifting a fish out of water and giving them a helicopter view of the entire river. Once the fish knows that streams peters out in a lifeless desert, it knows which stream not to take.

By contrast, the fish can also see the branches of the river that lead to rich feeding ponds. The decision of which path to take, whether for the fish or the employee, is not so much a matter of being "taught" to make right choice as being "caught" by the big picture and understanding its implications. The eventual decision then becomes obvious.

Q: So the learning curve, especially for bright employees, takes place quite quickly?

Yes, but with a qualification. I'm not suggesting that seeing the big picture of the company provides all the business tools an employee will need for his or her rise within the company. It takes time to get to know the various parts of any large company and to navigate the inevitable politics and priorities among those parts.

Our goal at DHL was to equip new employees as soon as possible with the specific concepts, skills, and tools they would need to hit (or hopefully exceed) their assigned performance targets. The lessons they learn at this lower edge of the learning curve (for example, an understanding of "zero defect," "customer focus," "industry experience curve," and "value added") stick with them as their responsibility and rank increase.

They use all they have learned along the way not only to improve their own performance and that of those they supervise, but also to locate and exploit the weaknesses of competitors.

Q: Describe one such weakness of a competitor. We can keep names out of it.

Gladly. Many successful DHL leaders have told me that their careers with the company really began to take off when they "understood their customers' pain." That may sound like an overly dramatic way to state a business idea, but I believe it is both accurate and appropriate.

Customers by and large are not independently wealthy and working simply as a whim or for something to occupy themselves. Their lives and aspirations (including what they hope to build for their families) hang on the day-to-day success of the enterprise in which they are involved.

Their "pain" occurs when obstacles interrupt the success of that enterprise. Let's say they have the opportunity to buy or rent an adjoining office space from an out-of-country owner. Their success in closing this transaction will depend directly on their ability to acquire in a timely way the legal documents they need for the deal.

Or they may be able to make a large sale, if only they can receive shipment of the desired goods by a specific date. To miss any of these deadlines is "pain" in the form of potential enterprise failure for the customer.

At DHL, we want our people to "get inside the skins" of their customers to the point that their pain becomes ours. When they feel extraordinary pressure to expedite a shipment, package, or document, we want our people to feel that pressure as well. The worst thing a courier can show to a panicked customer is a yawn and a "your problem" attitude.

Therefore, one weakness revealed by some competitors is a rushed, impersonal attitude communicated by their employees. A company like DHL can achieve competitive advantage simply by following the adage made famous by Avis: "We try harder." The roots of trying harder, of course, lie in knowing (and feeling) the customer's dilemma and resolving to do everything possible to help solve it.

Q: What you've described sounds like a company on a mission—but a mission that transcends its own business interests. The mission deeply involves the customer's interests as well.

Absolutely. Mission statements, of course, go through periodic restatements and revisions. But one version of the DHL Mission Statement, I believe, is worth quoting here. It will sum up much of our discussion about how and why the company decentralizes its authority and focuses on the world as seen through the customer's eyes.

Here's the Mission Statement to which I refer:

"DHL will become the acknowledged global leader in the express delivery of documents and packages.

Leadership will be achieved by establishing the industry standards of excellence for quality of service and by maintaining the lowest cost position relative to our service commitment in all markets of the world.

Achievement of the mission requires:

–Absolute dedication to understanding and fulfilling our customers' needs with the appropriate mix of service, reliability, products and price for each customer.

–Ensuring the long-term success of the business through profitable growth and re-investment of earnings.

–An environment that rewards achievement, enthusiasm, and team spirit and which offers each person in DHL superior opportunities for personal development and growth.

–A state-of-the-art worldwide information network for customer service and management information/communicating.

–Allocation of resources consistent with the recognition that we are one worldwide business.

–A professional organization able to maintain local initiative and local decision-making while working together within a centrally managed network.

–The evolution of our business into new services, markets, or products will be completely driven by our single-minded commitment to anticipating and meeting the changing needs of our customers."

It is of utmost importance to understand that this ambitious mission is impossible to achieve only with top-down, centralized leadership. The success of this kind of mission-driven company can only be achieved through a distributed top-down, bottom-up, and side-to-side model of leadership.

Q: *Some companies get their annual shot in the arm by a rousing speech by the CEO or President at a national conference. How would you describe DHL's way of "staying young," if you wish—that is, keeping nimble and avoiding the lure of resting on one's laurels.*

Although we also use inspirational speeches and other communications to rally the troops, our primary mechanism for systematic revitalization is the annual budget preparation. Let me tell you about it in detail, since it can easily be adapted and may suggest a revitalization process for other companies.

The budget preparation process typically starts in July with a global meeting. Sixty senior managers from all over the globe get together and decide such factors as where, what, who and how with regard to the customers and the competitive factors facing the company.

Unencumbered by tradition, budget and cost, strategic issues are discussed and decisions are made as to what should be done to strengthen DHL, especially how to offer it as an eventual better business solution and a superior choice to services offered by the competition.

The assembled group of senior managers talk about the three C's—the Company, the Competition, and our Customers. They analyze our environment for business, how the company addresses the needs of those environments, and how we view ourselves as a company. We not only score ourselves as an enterprise but also attempt to give an objective score to our competitors as well.

With strategic guidelines established at this meeting, each regional managing director then asks his or her country team to develop localized business plans while keeping the global goals and guidelines in mind.

By September, a budget is built bottom-up, based on the specific country business plans.

The budgeting package includes all the strategic elements of how the country addresses its customers, plans for service improvements, and deals with competition and costs.

At this stage, the package becomes both a strategic document and a financial document.

By November, the budget review process occurs. The budget review is, in fact, a formality, but it is very different from the budget process of many other companies. For example, our head office goes to the field for budget review. At most companies, the field managers and supervisors are called to the head office.

Because the budget is prepared at the supervisor's level, our managerial staff teaches strategy. They use strategic education while building the budget. "Why are we doing this?" becomes a common mantra as the budget-building process goes forth.

This kind of revitalization process takes place each year, forcing us to look at our customers in a new light, to see our products and ourselves as realistically as possible, and to reaffirm our commitment that no one else in the industry can "express it better."

Q: Related to the corporate revitalization you've described is personal revitalization—the energy or boost that each employee needs to receive periodically to keep motivation and job satisfaction high.

And in this area I think DHL has always scored highly. Many companies use a shotgun approach to their treatment of employees. In the same global firm, employees in one division may exist uncomfortably under a tyrant while in another division rewards seem to be passed out without rhyme or reason.

In a rational, well-run organization, operational relationships have to proceed from a central concept, principle, or model. At DHL, that model is the family. That master metaphor dictates the nature of all our employee relationships.

For example, we don't disown anyone because of inadvertent mistakes. The key thing is to maintain a company atmosphere of safety where people can talk freely both about their successes and mistakes, always with an eye towards making the company better.

Treating employees like family members means giving them basic assurances. In a family, the mother is not disowned for cooking an occasional bad meal. A son is not banished because of a low test score. Once they understand that they live at the heart of the organization instead of tenuously at its margins, employees can focus on doing their best to preserve and nurture the organization (or family).

When the organization is threatened (let's say by a price war from competitors), the employees act out of loyalty (much like family loyalty) to contain costs, make budget cuts, or go the extra mile to demonstrate superior customer service as a way of besting the competition.

Q: But surely you have to fire people from time to time, even in the happiest of family environments?

We begin with the assumption that all employees will be treated as members of our huge global family. We want it to be difficult to fire employees and we want every manager to ask why such action is necessary and what precipitated it.

Our goal, therefore, is to catch job-threatening behaviors early and intervene in a positive, coaching role. After all, the rest of the workforce is watching, and nothing spreads faster on the employee grapevine than a dismissal poorly or unjustly handled. According to Baumeister et al., "bad is stronger than good" as a general principle across a wide range of psychological phenomena. This blunt phrase can be interpreted to mean that a company should get rid of "bad apples" if your caring interventions don't work. Other employees may appreciate your efforts to save the bad apple, but not taking decisive action following failure might be catastrophic. Other members of the group will soon view a team member who consistently undermines the competitiveness of the group as an outsider.

Simply on a practical level, it makes far more business sense to "save" a marginal employee by effective intervention than to go through a messy, unsympathetic firing (with potential litigation) and the inevitability of mistakes on the part of a new hire to replace the terminated employee.

In short, we do whatever we can to prevent termination, although sometimes it is necessary. We consider it our last resort, not our first option.

That being said, while DHL tried to hire character and care and train skills, occasionally they made a mistake. When this happened, an over-riding policy was <u>not</u> to promote highly skilled people who came up short in terms of character or care as they could do more damage upstairs in the organization. The company sidelined them to a position where they could do no damage. Not promoting them reinforced the notion that character and care were critical and that even minor indiscretions, while not terminable, were costly to the employee in terms of remuneration and advancement.

DHL is not the first company, of course, to conceive of itself as a family. That organizing metaphor is still used by Disney throughout the world, although many Disney employees will assert that, once employed by Disney, the "family" is dysfunctional indeed in its various hierarchies of management.

By using the term family, I am not intending to diminish the ultimately important bond that grows up within actual families—for many of us, the reason we get up each morning. Although my employee is not literally my son or daughter, the point is that I urge myself to care for his or her interests and development as if they were in a family relationship with me. I want the best for them. I focus on helping them achieve their goals.

The concept of family, I suggest, can be an aspirational model for any organization. It does not prevent appropriate discipline, any more than in real family dynamics. Nor does it blur levels of authority and responsibility. But it does engender a "safety zone"—a place one can "come home to" after both good and bad days in the working world. That feeling of safety leads to low turnover, high performance, strong loyalty to co-workers and the company, and a sincere passion to help the organization succeed.

Q: Po, I think I would like to be a member of your professional family.

The application forms are on-line!

Q: Thank you for this opportunity to talk at length about your perspective on age-old problems: how to get people to work together for the common good, including the common good found in professional life.

I enjoyed our chat.

KEY POINTS

1. The concept of "operate" includes an appropriate connotation of "taking pains, exertion, labor." Company leaders take on a profound responsibility in relation to those they employ. An emotional component is inevitably involved in concerned leadership.

2. Employees at their best perform more like orchestral conductors than as cogs in a machine. They are sensitive to their business environment, adaptive to their audience, and committed to making harmony, not noise, in their business lives.

3. So that employees do not get the idea they can "park their brains at the door" each day, it is good business practice to drive decision-making to the lowest level. The ability to handle responsibility grows in direct correlation with the opportunity to demonstrate responsibility.

4. The organization should commit itself to teaching strategic thinking to all employees. When employees grasp the "Why?" that undergirds company decisions, they are better equipped to make good decisions on their own as well as to spot weaknesses in the competition.

5. Mistakes are most dangerous when they are hidden. In a work culture that views occasional mistakes as opportunities for organizational learning, mistakes should be discussed openly so that others can avoid these problems.

6. Employees are best viewed as riding an upward-bound escalator, not spinning in a perpetual hamster wheel. Employees are willing to give loyalty and top performance to the organization that gives to them in the form of opportunities for growth and development.

7. The key to handling many emergency situations lies in forging a wide and deep network of relationships. In a "people world," work-around solutions can often be found that aren't in the rulebooks.

8. The term "empowerment" implies a giving-over of power from upper authority to lower levels. A better and more accurate term applicable to many successful organizations is "decentralized authority," in which power is appropriately distributed among levels of hierarchy.

9. Decentralized authority must be dispensed carefully and a bit at a time, so as not to overwhelm employees unused to making large-scale or particularly important decisions.

10. The best "managers" are in fact "entrepreneurs" inside or outside their organizations, as demonstrated by their creativity, willingness to experiment, tolerance of occasional mistakes, and optimism.

11. Employees who become "caught up" in seeing the big picture of company aspirations and endeavors are adept at spotting strategic deadends as well as strategic opportunities.

12. Organizations can achieve substantial competitive advantage by making the effort to "understand their customers' pain"—that is, empathizing with the pressures and challenges faced by their customers and doing everything they can to respond in a helpful way to those difficulties.

13. The budget process, as illustrated at DHL, can be an extremely useful exercise in strategic thinking and corporate revitalization, especially when "the field" is welcomed into the discussion in bottom-up budget creation.

14. Personal revitalization for individual workers can come through the company's commitment to a set of family values in which every member is valued, respected, appropriately praised, disciplined in a developmental spirit, and allowed to reveal and discuss mistakes without fear of banishment.

Epilogue

The conversations that make up this book took place over a period of weeks in Spring, 2011. Art Bell and I would typically meet over dinner and well into the evening to talk in depth about the status of service occupations in Hong Kong and throughout the world, the nature of service leadership, the roles of educational institutions in preparing students for service careers, and countless related topics.

In these conversations, which Art has handily stitched together into a single dialogue making up this book, I more than once called to mind the shrewd observation of the famed linguist Deborah Tannen: "Each person's life is lived as a series of conversations." I realized, as my conversation with Art took various twists and turns, that I was in fact setting forth a "life" or autobiography of sorts—my life, my experience in service leadership, and my commitment to those I serve. Bound up in our mutual sharing of ideas were the main passions, principles, and practices that had animated my professional and personal life.

Could the conversation have continued? Of course. Since his return from his year in Hong Kong to the U.S., Art has no doubt thought of new questions to pose and new perspectives to explore. My thinking and teaching about service leadership has similarly evolved, especially with regard to the roll-out in Hong Kong of service leadership curricula in the city's eight major universities, with support from the Victor and William Fung Foundation.

But in spite of this natural evolution of continuing insight, I am happy to offer *Service Reborn* to readers as a balanced, well-considered, and I hope interesting compilation of my central thoughts on service leadership through mid-2012. I stand by the overarching proposition that service occupations matter intensely not only to the economy and people of Hong Kong but to centers of commerce and government throughout the world. I remain passionate in my goal of seeing service leadership curricula established in our schools and universities as a respected and popular field of study, as we prepare students for their future, not our past.

John Mason Brown, the renowned drama critic and journalist, remarked that "a good conversationalist is not one who remembers what was said, but says what someone wants to remember." In my prolonged, enjoyable conversations with Art Bell, I tried to bear in mind that I was in fact talking *through* him to a larger, international audience of service leaders, service providers, managers, managers-in-training, and their professors. I endeavored, therefore, not simply to engage in topical, useful chat but to deliver, in Brown's phrase, "what someone wants to remember." It is my fervent hope that the ideas punctuating our conversation take on a life of their own, spawning new and deep reflection about service leadership in the modern world.

As this conversation draws to a formal close with the publication of *Service Reborn*, new conversations have already begun, with new projects underway, and new challenges on the horizon. But I take this moment to reflect that in *Service Reborn* my service to others has emerged as a story about my own service leadership roles, about DHL, about East and West, and about what I have learned. I trust that my story will turn out to be its own service to readers—a parable of sorts, as they reflect on the local and global importance of service roles, service organizations, and service leadership to themselves, their economies, their societies, and our shared world.

Po Chung
Hong Kong, June, 2012

As I add my brief "Amen" to Po's epilogue, let me recall the words of Greek dramatist and philosopher Menander: "The character of a man is known through his conversations." It was indeed my privilege to spend cherished hours of conversation with Po Chung. In these intense, stimulating engagements, I came to know the character of the man behind the legend of DHL's leader in Asia—a man committed to sharing the fruit of his amazing professional and civic life with those already on the path to service leadership or simply taking the first tentative steps on that journey.

In conveying these conversations faithfully and, to the extent of my abilities, catching up Po Chung's voice, passion, and insight in these pages, I owe an immense debt of gratitude to this friend and mentor not only for the time he devoted to our mutual project but especially for his patience and kindness in helping me understand and appreciate new ideas, ethical priorities, and best practices in service leadership. Po and I continue to talk regularly. And yes, I am taking notes.

Art Bell, PhD
Business Editor
Lexingford Publishing
June, 2012

Resources Referenced and Recommended

Note: latest editions are listed wherever available.

Adams, Henry. The Dynamo and the Virgin. The Education of Henry Adams. Amazon Digital Services, 2009.

Adams, J. Stacy. Interviewing Procedures. University of North Carolina Press, 2011.

Armstrong, Sharon. The Essential HR Handbook. Career Press, 2008.

Badaracco, Joseph. Questions of Character: Illuminating the Heart of Leadership through Literature. Harvard Business Review Press, 2006.

Baumeister, Roy. Advanced Social Psychology: the State of the Science. Oxford University Press, 2010.

Baumeister, Roy et al. "Bad is Stronger than Good. Review of General Psychology (2001), Vo. 5, No. 4, 323-370.

Behan, Beverly. Great Companies Deserve Great Boards. Palgrave Macmillan, 2011.

Bell, Arthur and Dayle Smith. Management Communication. Wiley, 2010.

Bell, Arthur et al. Winning with Difficult People, 3e. Barron's, 2003.

Bennis, Warren. On Becoming a Leader. Basic Books, 2009.

Bruce, Loeffler. One Minute Service: Keys to Providing Great Service Like Disney World. DC Press, 2009.

Burns, James. Leadership. Harper, 2010.

Chen, Chao-Chuan et al. Leadership and Management in China: Philosophies, Theories, and Practices. Cambridge University Press, 2008.

Chung, Po. The First Ten Yards: The 5 Dynamics of Entrepreneurship. Cengage, 2008.

Dent, Christopher M. China, Japan, and Regional Leadership in East Asia. Edward Elgar, 2010.

Diamond, Jared. Guns, Germs, and Steel: the Fates of Human Societies. W.W. Norton, 2005.

Dominguez, Joseph and Vicki Robin. Your Money or Your Life. Penguin, 2003.

Drucker, Peter. The Effective Executive: the Definite Guide to Getting the Right Things Done. Harper, 2006.

Drucker, Peter. The Essential Drucker. Collins, 2008.

Eco, Umberto. The Name of the Rose. Everyman's Library, 2006.

Essany, Michael. Steve Jobs: Ten Lessons in Leadership. New Beginnings, 2012.

Finkelstein, Stanley. Why Smart Executives Fail. Portfolio Trade, 2004.

Fiorina, Carly. Tough Choices: a Memoir. Portfolio Trade, 2007.

Gad, Thomas. 4-D Branding: Cracking the Corporate Code of the Network Economy. Prentice Hall, 2000.

Gad, Thomas and Anette Rosencreutz. Managing Brand Me: How to Build Your Personal Brand. Pearson, 2002.

Gallo, Frank T. Business Leadership in China: How to Blend Best Western Practices with Chinese Wisdom. Wiley, 2011.

Godin, Seth. Tribes: We Need You to Lead Us. Portfolio Trade, 2008.

Goleman, Daniel. Primal Leadership: Learning to Lead with Emotional Intelligence. Harvard Business School Press, 2004.

Goodwin, Doris. Team of Rivals. Simon & Schuster, 2006.

Greenleaf, Robert et al. Servant Leadership: A Journey into the Nature of Legitimate Power and Greatness. Paulist Press, 2002.

Gronfeldt, Svafa et al. Service Leadership: The Quest for Competitive Advantage. Sage, 2005.

Grulke, Wolfgang. 10 Lessons from the Future: Tomorrow is a Matter of Choice. Make It Your Own. Financial Times, 2000.

Hackman, Michael et al. Leadership: A Communication Perspective. Waveland Press, 2008.

Hamm, John. Unusually Excellent: The Necessary Nine Skills Required for the Practice of Great Leadership. Jossey-Bass, 2011.

Hawkins, Bradley. Asian Religions: An Illustrated Introduction. Longman's, 2003.

Inghilleri, Leonardo et al., Exceptional Service, Exceptional Profit: The Secrets of Building a Five-Star Customer Service Organization. AMACOM, 2010.

Kim, W. Chan and Renee Mauborgne. Blue Ocean Strategy: How to Create Uncontested Market Space and Make Competition Irrelevant. Harvard Business School Press, 2005.

Kotler, Philip. Principles of Marketing. 14th edition. Prentice Hall, 2011.

Levene, Malcolm. 10 Steps to Fashion Freedom. Crown, 2001.

Maslow, Abraham. Toward a Psychology of Being. Wiley, 1998.

Maxwell, John. The 21 Irrefutable Laws of Leadership. Nelson, 2007.

Magretta, Joan. What Management Is: How It Works and Why It's Everyone's Business. Free Press, 2002.

Manning, Susan. Ethical Leadership in Human Services: A Multi-Dimensional Approach. Allyn & Bacon, 2002.

McGregor, Douglas. The Human Side of Enterprise. Annotated Edition. McGraw Hill, 2005.

Michelli, Joseph. Prescription for Excellence: Leadership Lessons for Creating a World Class Customer Experience from the UCLA Health System. McGraw Hill, 2011.

Mintzberg, Henry. The Rise and Fall of Strategic Planning. Pearson, 2000.

Morgan, Gareth. Images of Organizations. Sage, 2006.

Northouse, Peter. Leadership: Theory and Practice. Sage, 2009.

James O'Toole. Good Business: Exercising Effective and Ethical Leadership. Routledge, 2010.

Pink, Daniel. Drive: the Truth about What Motivate Us. Riverhead, 2011.

Porras, Jerry et al. Success Built to Last. Plume, 2007.

Rath, Tom et al. Strengths-Based Leadership. Gallup Press, 2009.

Ries, Al and Jack Trout. The 22 Immutable Laws of Marketing. Harper, 1994.

Robinson, Joseph. Work to Live: The Guide to Getting a Life. Perigee, 2003.

Ross, Stephen et al. Fundamentals of Corporate Finance. McGraw Hill, 2010.

Rumelt, Richard. Good Strategy, Bad Strategy. Crown, 2011.

Shaban, Fuad. For Zion's Sake: The Judeo-Christian Tradition in American Culture. Pluto Press, 2005.

Sipe, James and Don Frick. Seven Pillars of Servant Leadership: Practicing the Wisdom of Leading by Serving. Paulist Press, 2009.

Smith, Dayle et al. Why Should I? Ten Keys to Motivating People. Lexingford, 2010.

Smith, Dayle. Motivating People. Barron's, 1997.

Spillane, Mary. Branding Yourself: How to Look, Sound, and Behave Your Way to Success. Macmillan, 2000.

Taylor, Frederick Winslow. Principles of Scientific Management. Republication. CreateSpace, 2011.

Tannen, Deborah. Talking from Nine to Five: Men and Women at Work. Morrow, 1995.

Terrill, Craig et al. Market Leadership Strategies for Service Companies. McGraw Hill, 1999.

Tolstoy, Leo. Anna Karenina. Republication. Simon & Brown, 2011.

Townsend, Robert. Up the Organization. Jossey-Bass, 2007.

Trilling, Lionel. The Liberal Imagination. Republication. NYRB, 2008.

Van Wart, Montgomery. Dynamics of Leadership in Public Service: Theory and Practice. Sharpe, 2011.

Vroom, Victor. Work and Motivation. Jossey-Bass, 1994.

Weber, Max. The Protestant Work Ethic and the Spirit of Capitalism. Republication. Penguin, 2002.

Worthley, Brad. Outstanding Leadership in a Service Culture. Made for Success, 2008.

Yuan, Fangyuan and Meiru Liu. Anatomy of the Chinese Business Mind: an Insider's Perspective. Cengage, 2008.

Notes

1 Fiske, Susan T., Amy J.C. Cuddy, and Peter Glick. Universal Dimension of Social Cognition: Warmth and Competence. Trends in Cognitive Science. Vol. 11, No. 2. 77-83.

2 McGregor, Douglas. The Human Side of Enterprise. Annotated edition. McGraw Hill, 2005. McGregor describes "Theory X" managers as authoritarian bosses who manage primarily through disciplinary measures and fear.

3 This work philosophy is elaborated in Frederick Taylor's Principles of Scientific Management (1911).

4 Po Chung makes reference here to Frederick Taylor's influential theories of scientific management, otherwise known as the Efficiency Movement. An eloquent rebuttal to Taylor came in Henry Mintzberg's seminal work, The Rise and Fall of Strategic Planning (Mintzberg 1994). He demonstrates that, while some companies (in Mintzberg's terms, "Machine Companies") may achieve some advantage by work standardization and limitation of worker creativity, there are other, equally valid forms of habitat-building that result in what Mintzberg called the Innovative Company and the Diversified Company.

5 For Western readers, a guide to the main texts from Buddhism, Confucianism, and Taoism is included in the Resources section of this

book. For Eastern readers, a similar set of suggested readings are provided for principal Protestant, Catholic, and Jewish theologies.

6 The phrase occurs in the poem, "Kubla Khan," by Samuel Taylor Coleridge.

7 The remark is attributed to Branch Rickey, general manager of the Brooklyn Dodgers.

8 This citation appears in Jerry Porras, Success Built to Last (Plume, 2007), p. 27.

9 Full citations for these works appear in the Resources section of this book.

10 Research summarized in Smith et al., Why Should I? Ten Keys to Motivating People. Lexingford Publishing, 2010. P. 84.

11 The essential ideas contained in Maslow's hierarchy of needs have been rendered in various terms and graphics in keeping with his intent in their original appearance in his 1943 paper, "A Theory of Human Motivation." See Maslow, A.H. (1943). "A Theory of Human Motivation," Psychological Review 50(4): 370-96.

12 See David C. McClelland, "Methods of Measuring Human Motivation", in John W. Atkinson, ed., Motives in Fantasy, Action and Society (Princeton, N.J.: D. Van Nostrand, 1958), pp. 12–13.

13 See Vroom, Victor. Work and Motivation. Jossey-Bass, 1994.

14 This formulation was originally proposed by J. Stacy Adams. His research is well summarized in Smith et al., Motivating People. Barron's, 1997.

15 Dominguez, Joseph and Vicki Robin. Your Money or Your Life. Penguin, 2003

16 Research relating the Dartmouth Heart Study to executive and managerial stress appears in Arthur Bell and Dayle Smith, Winning with Difficult People, 3e, Barron's, 2003.

Index

King Arthur 35
Kouzes, James 9

Leadership, fishnet 32, 42
Leadership, service role 9
Leadership, selling role 10
Leadership Challenge, The 9
Lockheed Martin 67
Locus 64-67
London 4, 19
Lovejoy, A.O. 33

Magretta, Joan 106
MacDonald's 107
MacGregor, Douglas 34, 104
Mandelbrot, Benoit 63
Mary Kay Cosmetics 65-66
Maslow, Abraham 84
Maxwell, John 6
Me, Incorporated 106-110
Mentor-apprentice 105
Mission 29, 143-144
Moral virus 18-19
Morale 31
Motivation 81-92
Myers-Briggs Type Inventory
  (MBTI) 22

Name of the Rose, The 11
New York City 4, 43

Operate (business) 131-148
OS-X 19
Oxford English Dictionary 23, 131

Paris 4

People skills 6, 9
Pepsi Company 103, 116
Personal Operating System, POS
  17, 21, 22, 97, 99
Personal Software Acquisition, PSA
  99
Plato 97
Porras, Jerry 62
POS, Personal Operating System
  17, 97-101
Posner, Barry 9
Product skills 9
Prometheus Unbound 29

Rank of sensitivity 7
Ries, Al 111
Roosevelt, Theodore 6
Rosencreutz, Anette 112

San Francisco 4
Scandinavian Airlines 47
Service (business) 1-23
Service, definition of 3
Service, forms of 2, 3
Service leader 32
Service revolution 23
Service, status of 3
Seven Pillars of Servant Leadership 32
Shanghai 43
Shelley, Percy Bysshe 29
Singapore 4
Sipe, James 32
Sistine Chapel 63
Soft skills 8
Spillane, Mary 111
Star Wars 91

www.ingramcontent.com/pod-product-compliance
Lightning Source LLC
Chambersburg PA
CBHW072347200326
41519CB00015B/3691